THE STORY OF
THE BIBLE

VOLUME I
THE OLD TESTAMENT

Teacher's Manual

Copyright © 2015 TAN Books, PO Box 410487, Charlotte, NC 28241.

All rights reserved. No part of this book may be reproduced or transmitted in any form or by any means, electronic or mechanical, including photocopying, recording, or by any information storage or retrieval system, without permission in writing from the publisher, except that brief selections may be quoted or copied for non-profit use without permission.

Cataloging-in-Publication data on file with the Library of Congress.

Illustrations by Chris Pelicano, Caroline Kiser, and askib/shutterstock.

ISBN: 978-1-61890-671-7

Printed and bound in the United States of America

THE STORY OF THE BIBLE

VOLUME I
THE OLD TESTAMENT

Teacher's Manual

TAN

CONTENTS

A Word to the Teacher 9

Activity Materials at a Glance 15

Introduction: Your Time Has Come 29

PART ONE: How God Came to Promise Us a Redeemer

    Chapter 1: In the Beginning 31

    Chapter 2: The Descendants of Adam and Eve 39

PART TWO: How God Founded the Nation From Which the Redeemer of the World Came

    Chapter 3: Abraham and Isaac 45

    Chapter 4: Jacob, the Son of Isaac 49

    Chapter 5: Joseph, the Son of Jacob 53

PART THREE: How God Protected His Chosen People and Led Them Into the Promised Land

    Chapter 6: God Calls Moses to Lead His People 59

    Chapter 7: The Escape From Egypt 63

    Chapter 8: The Revelation of God's Law 69

    Chapter 9: The Desert Wanderings of the Israelites 75

    Chapter 10: Joshua, Commander of the Israelites 79

    Chapter 11: The Israelites in the Promised Land 83

PART FOUR: How God's Chosen People Lived Under Their Kings

    Chapter 12: Saul and David 89

    Chapter 13: David's Reign 93

    Chapter 14: The Israelites Under King Solomon 97

    Chapter 15: Jeroboam and Rehoboam 101

    Chapter 16: Elijah the Prophet 105

    Chapter 17: The Stories of Job and Jonah 109

PART FIVE: How God's People Went Into Exile and Returned

    Chapter 18: The Assyrian Invasions 115

    Chapter 19: Daniel and the Babylonian Captivity 119

    Chapter 20: The Prophets 125

    Chapter 21: The Return to Jerusalem 129

    Chapter 22: The Last Days of the Kingdom of Judah 133

And the Word became flesh and dwelt among us, full of grace and truth; we have beheld his glory, glory as of the only Son from the Father.

— John 1:14

THE OLD TESTAMENT

HOW TO USE THIS TEACHER'S MANUAL

Teaching Bible History

History is at the core of any classical education. Engaging in the study of history gives children and adults a context for the world in which we live. Learning the great triumphs and failures of previous generations helps mold the decisions we make today. Bible History in particular is necessary for a solid education.

Why is Bible History so important? Salvation! Study of the Bible is an attempt to better understand the Creator, the reason for creation, and its ultimate destination. In studying the Bible we come to know God better. In knowing Him better we begin to love Him more. The more we love Him, the more we will serve Him. Knowing, loving, and serving God will lead us to happiness with Him for eternity. Isn't this the whole point?

Now, here are some more worldly reasons to study the Bible. Yes, worldly. The benefits of biblical study aren't simply confined to religion or to history. Take literature for an example. Can you imagine reading Milton without an understanding of the Bible? How about Dante, Dostoyevsky, or Shakespeare? This list is inexhaustible! No book has made a greater impact on world literature than the Bible.

What about art and music? The world's greatest artists have had the Bible as their muse. What would viewing the Sistine Chapel be like without knowledge of Bible History? Without proper context it has no meaning! The same is true for the works of Rembrandt, da Vinci, Caravaggio, and countless others. The famous works of Bach, Mozart, Vivaldi, Haydn, and so many others were likewise inspired by the dramatic stories of the Bible.

What about the American legal system? Should children be taught about the laws of government? Should they be familiar with the constitution of the country? Of course! But to do so they must first be familiar with the biblical roots of our legal system.

God is the author of creation. He created and set forth the laws of nature. He is the reason that music touches the soul, that art is inspirational, that literature brings such great pleasure. To bypass the study of Him is to be culturally illiterate!

Teaching Using the One-Room Schoolhouse Model

The Story of the Bible is a wonderful text for teaching a single student or for teaching many students of varying grades all at one time. This text is designed to be used for grades 1–8.

If you are using this text with younger grades, you should revisit it again when the student is older. A classical education depends on laying a broad foundation at a young age that will be expanded upon later. Using *Story of the Bible* twice will enhance the student's knowledge of the Bible and allow for the addition of detail in later grades that was not committed to memory in early ones.

Using a schoolhouse model is not something seen in brick and mortar schools today, but it was the standard in the very recent past . . . and it worked. Some home schools utilize this method out of necessity or convenience. Some do so intentionally because they find it to be a superior pedagogical method. Regardless of the reasoning, the one room schoolhouse model works and works well.

If you use the schoolhouse model, your older students might enjoy sitting in and following along in their own book while you read to the younger students. Older students then have the opportunity to review on their own. Going over *Questions for Review* as a group provides older students with a chance to help younger students with forgotten facts and provides younger students with the opportunity to show off what they know in front of older students. Impressing the parent or teacher is often not nearly as enticing as impressing an older sibling or student. Likewise, learning something for your own sake may not be as enticing as sharing what you have learned with someone else.

If you are only using this text with students of the same age, the schoolhouse model can still be of great benefit. A little healthy competition can bring many children out of their shells and provide incentive for paying attention.

Using this Teacher's Manual

This Teacher's Manual is meant to work in conjunction with the Activity Book that goes along with the *Story of the Bible: Old Testament* series. The activities contained in this book are to be used after your student has completed the chapter of the text book. The following is a list of sections you will find in this Teacher's Manual and the age range for which each section is appropriate:

LISTENING TO GOD'S WORD

This section of the Teacher's Manual is appropriate for middle school students. Have the student look up the biblical verse or passage provided and read it for himself. Next, have the student spend a few minutes meditating on the verse or passage. Then the student should use the passage to focus his prayer. As he reads each verse of the passage, he should ask himself these questions to help him know how to pray:

1. Does this passage give me a prayer to pray?
2. Does this passage show me a person who can teach me something about how to pray?
3. Does this passage tell me something about God that leads me to thank and praise Him?
4. Does this passage bring to mind anything that I need to pray about, such as a challenge, a worry or fear, something God has done for me, something I've done wrong, or something God wants me to do?

You may want to have the student conclude the prayer with an Our Father, a Hail Mary, and a Glory Be.

Contemplation is the final step. Ask the child to take some time after prayer to simply take it all in. This is the resting step where you just open yourself to God and what He wants to tell you.

This exercise not only leads students to pray but also helps them become familiar with the Bible and learn how to find specific passages.

QUESTIONS FOR REVIEW

This section is beneficial for the full range of elementary and middle school grades. For early elementary students, this section should be completed orally with lots of prompting and helpful hints. If you find the child struggling to come up with the answers independently, it may be most beneficial to both read the questions and provide the answers while engaging in discussion. Mastery of the answers should not be expected at these young ages. Exposure to the concepts is the key. For later elementary school students, an oral evaluation is recommended. Expect *most* of the details to be provided by the student with minimal prompting. Oral answers should be given in complete sentences. For the middle school grades, a written evaluation would be ideal. Again, expect the student to provide *most* of the details. If you are teaching both elementary and middle school grades together, use the questions as an oral review for all, allowing the older students to aid the younger students with the details. Then use the questions as a written review for the older students, and at this point expect very good written responses since the questions have already been reviewed orally.

NARRATION EXERCISES

This section is most beneficial for the elementary aged student. Ask the student to provide you with a brief summary of the chapter. For the early elementary grades, expect knowledge of the basic storyline and provide any details that the child has omitted. For later elementary grades, the story line should be supplied by the student. An example is been provided for each chapter. This is just an example, not something that needs to be duplicated exactly by the student. You may want to have older elementary students keep a written account of their own responses. If desired, the teacher can produce and keep a written account for younger students.

MAP ACTIVITIES

This section is beneficial for the full range of elementary and middle school students. It is meant to provide a visual reference for the location in which the stories take place. It is helpful to make use of a world map from time to time to remind the student of the overall world placement of the events before honing in on the particulars of the exact locale. This Teacher's Manual provides directions for each map activity. The maps are located in the Activity Book under the chapter that corresponds with this text. You will find a map activity for almost every chapter.

ACTIVITY PROJECTS

There are a variety of Activity Projects found in this Teacher's Manual, each suited to different ages and interests. Please note that *not* all of the activities should be completed for each chapter. Choose the activities that will most engage your students, which will in turn fix the stories in their minds. Also note that a Materials at a Glance section has been added to the front of this manual so that you can gather your materials in advance without having to flip through each chapter. The possibilities of activities include:

COLORING PAGES

These are found with every chapter. Most of the pictures correspond with the pictures in the textbook. Visual representation for each chapter helps the student identify the events more clearly. Some coloring pages are purposefully designed to be more elaborate than a traditional coloring page. The lines aren't as clean, and there is a lot more detail. This makes these coloring pages ideal for the full range of elementary students as well as middle school students. Especially in the early elementary years, it is helpful to give out the coloring page before you begin reading the chapter. Allowing the child to work on the coloring page while the chapter is read keeps idle hands busy and brings to life the stories they are hearing.

WORD SEARCH AND CROSSWORD PUZZLES

These are designed for upper elementary and middle school students. If you have an early reader and proficient speller, younger students can attempt them, but their purpose is to provide a fun activity for the older students. The crossword or word search puzzles can be found in the Activity Book and the answer key is found in the corresponding chapters in this Teacher's Manual.

CRAFT PROJECTS

These are mostly designed for the elementary school student, although older students may find them fun as well. Gauge your student's interest level in doing the crafts. DO NOT force these crafts on uninterested students. History is supposed to be fun and these crafts are designed to support that idea, not to become one more activity to have to do on top of all the other school work! Directions for each craft can be found under the appropriate chapter.

SNACK PROJECTS

Now who doesn't love a good snack? And in some cases a full meal? This section is for use by any age (including adults). The snack provides another link to the Bible story and helps reinforce the chapter. Weeks or even months later when you ask for the story of Jacob and Esau, for example, and your 2nd grader looks at you with a blank stare, you can say, "Remember the soup we made?" and click, the connection is made and full story retold.

SCIENCE PROJECTS

These are intended for upper elementary and middle school students. With a lot of help and supervision, early elementary students will also find these projects engaging. Again, the point is to reinforce the chapter and provide a hands-on project to help commit the stories to memory.

THE 5 KEYS TO MAKING THE MOST OF THIS TEACHER'S MANUAL

1. *Remember, history is fun!* Keep the classroom mood light. Allow your students a little room to engage, ask questions, and participate in discussions. Students shouldn't read this subject in order to get it over with as quickly as possible. It's meant to lay a foundation for a love of learning. Whether your students are in elementary grades, middle school grades, or a mixture of the two, this text in meant to engage them in deep thought. They are challenged to open their minds and stretch their imaginations, to travel back in time to trace the origins of the human race and of the universe itself! Please make sure the journey is a fun one.

2. *DO NOT, under any circumstances, attempt to do all the activities in this book!* It's simply too much. Pick the activities that you think will be most beneficial for your students and do those. If you find a chapter or two in which you think all the activities are doable and you find yourself with extra time on your hands, go for it. If you find that one week a coloring page and word search were all that you could manage, don't beat yourself up. This curriculum is designed to be fun for both the student and the teacher.

3. *Be a passenger on the voyage.* If, as the teacher, you learn something new or are reminded of something that you almost forgot, let your students see that you too are growing in knowledge. Allow your own excitement of the stories to come out in your discussion with the students. The best way to engage your student is to be engaged yourself.

4. *Don't set the bar too high for younger students.* As parent-teachers we are often tempted to expect too much of our children because we know they are capable of it. If you are using this text with early elementary students, you should revisit it when your children are older. Expose younger students to all the Bible has to offer, but don't try to drill every detail into them.

5. *If you have older students, let them take on some of the responsibility.* Let them look through the coming weeks and make a list of the activities they are most interested in. Allow them to list out and gather the supplies. If there are younger students in the classroom as well, allow the older students to pick out activities that they can help the younger students complete. Taking an active role in choosing the activities helps the student take ownership over what is learned.

Activity Materials at a Glance

Chapter 1

Craft Project 1: PAPER PLATE SNAKE WIND TWIRLER

Materials:

- ☐ paper plate
- ☐ any color washable paint for your snake
- ☐ hot glue gun
- ☐ red yarn
- ☐ craft googly eyes
- ☐ scissors

Craft Project 2: MAKE THE TREE OF KNOWLEDGE

Materials:

- ☐ empty toilet paper roll
- ☐ 6 in. cardboard square
- ☐ brown pipe cleaner
- ☐ brown and green craft
- ☐ paint brush
- ☐ red craft beads
- ☐ hot glue gun
- ☐ hole punch

Snack Project 1: DAY 3 OF CREATION SNACK

Ingredients:

- ☐ 6 cups of crispy rice cereal
- ☐ 1 (10 ounce) package of regular marshmallows OR 4 cups of mini marshmallows
- ☐ 3 tablespoons butter
- ☐ green food coloring
- ☐ blue food coloring
- ☐ any fruit (bananas, strawberries, blueberries, oranges, grapes . . . the more visible the seed the better).
- ☐ any vegetable (carrots, celery, broccoli . . . any variety of vegetable).

Snack Project 2: GARDEN OF EDEN PIZZA PIE

Ingredients:

- ☐ 1 1/4 cup white sugar
- ☐ 1 cup butter
- ☐ 3 egg yolks
- ☐ 1 teaspoon vanilla extract
- ☐ 2 1/2 cups all-purpose flour
- ☐ 1 teaspoon baking soda
- ☐ 1/2 teaspoon cream of tartar
- ☐ 1 (8 ounce) package of cream cheese, softened
- ☐ 1 (8 ounce) container of frozen whipped topping (thaw)
- ☐ dash of salt
- ☐ 1 tablespoon cornstarch
- ☐ 1/2 cup of orange juice
- ☐ 2 tablespoons lemon juice
- ☐ 1/4 cup water
- ☐ 1/2 teaspoon orange zest
- ☐ strawberries
- ☐ kiwi
- ☐ bananas
- ☐ blueberries
- ☐ mandarin slices

Science Project 1: SECOND DAY OF CREATION LAVA LAMP

Materials:

- ☐ wax paper OR plastic funnel
- ☐ vegetable oil OR canola oil
- ☐ blue food coloring
- ☐ 3/4 cup water
- ☐ Alka-Seltzer tablets
- ☐ 2 liter plastic bottle with lid (soda bottle)

Chapter 2

Craft Project 1: NOAH'S ARK

Materials:

- ☐ activity page from Activity Book
- ☐ scissors
- ☐ glue
- ☐ markers
- ☐ clear tape

Craft Project 2: CAIN THE FARMER AND ABEL THE SHEPHERD SPOON PEOPLE

Materials:

- ☐ 2, 10-inch wooden spoons
- ☐ small piece of scrap fabric (preferably a neutral color)
- ☐ Template from Activity Book
- ☐ brown pipe cleaner
- ☐ markers
- ☐ colored pencils
- ☐ hot glue gun
- ☐ scissors

Activity Materials at a Glance

Science Experiment 1: CAIN AND ABEL'S HEARTS

Materials:
- ☐ 2 clear glasses
- ☐ water
- ☐ white vinegar
- ☐ green food coloring
- ☐ baking soda

Snack Project 1: NOAH'S BANANA ARK

Ingredients:
- ☐ banana
- ☐ peanut butter
- ☐ animal crackers

Chapter 3

Craft Project 1: A TENT FOR ABRAM AND SARAI

Materials:
- ☐ 4-6 twigs, each 10-12 inches in length
- ☐ 2 rubber bands
- ☐ 24 in. square of brown fabric
- ☐ scissors

Craft Project 2: STARS IN THE SKY

Materials:
- ☐ 24 oz. or larger glass jar (pickle jar works great)
- ☐ piece of aluminum foil
- ☐ nail
- ☐ battery-operated tea light candle

Craft Project 3: A RAM FOR THE SACRIFICE

Materials:
- ☐ Template from the Activity Book
- ☐ cotton balls
- ☐ craft glue
- ☐ coloring pencils
- ☐ scissors

Chapter 4

Snack Project 1: JACOB AND ESAU HAM AND POTATO SOUP
8 SERVINGS

Ingredients:

- ☐ 4 cups diced potatoes
- ☐ 1/2 cup chopped celery
- ☐ 1 cup diced cooked ham
- ☐ 3 1/4 cups water
- ☐ 2 tablespoons chicken bouillon
- ☐ 6 tablespoons butter or margarine
- ☐ salt to taste
- ☐ pepper to taste
- ☐ 6 tablespoons all purpose flour
- ☐ 2 1/3 cups of milk
- ☐ green onions to garnish

Snack Project 2: JACOB'S LADDER

Ingredients:

- ☐ pretzel sticks
- ☐ mini marshmallows

Craft Project 1: JACOB AND ESAU SPOON PEOPLE

Materials:

- ☐ 2, 10 in. wooden craft spoons
- ☐ Templates from Activity Book
- ☐ scissors
- ☐ hot glue gun
- ☐ craft glue
- ☐ brown yarn
- ☐ markers

Chapter 5

Craft Project 1: JOSEPH'S COAT OF MANY COLORS

Materials:

- ☐ several colors of construction paper
- ☐ paper grocery bag
- ☐ scissors
- ☐ craft glue
- ☐ clear tape (for reinforcement if desired)

Craft Project 2: THE BUTLER AND THE BAKER SPOON PEOPLE

Materials:

- ☐ 2, 10 in. wooden craft spoons
- ☐ Templates from Activity Book
- ☐ hot glue gun
- ☐ scissors
- ☐ coloring pencils

Activity Materials at a Glance

Snack project 1: SACK OF GRAIN-OLA

Ingredients:

- ☐ 4 cups rolled oats
- ☐ 3/4 cup oat bran
- ☐ 3/4 cup ground flax seed
- ☐ 1/2 cup sunflower or pumpkin seeds
- ☐ 3/4 cup finely chopped pecans
- ☐ 3/4 cup finely chopped walnuts
- ☐ 1/4 cup brown sugar
- ☐ 1/4 cup and 2 tablespoons honey
- ☐ 4 tablespoons maple syrup
- ☐ 3/4 teaspoon salt
- ☐ 1/2 cup oil (you can use vegetable, canola, coconut, whatever your preferred baking oil is)
- ☐ 1 1/2 teaspoons cinnamon
- ☐ 1 1/2 teaspoon vanilla extract
- ☐ chocolate covered coins OR colored chocolate candies
- ☐ paper lunch bags

Chapter 6

Craft Project 1: MOSES' BASKET ON THE NILE

Materials:

- ☐ paper plate
- ☐ white muffin liner
- ☐ green construction paper
- ☐ modeling clay
- ☐ blue and brown markers
- ☐ stapler

Craft Project 2: BALANCE FROG FROM THE FROG PLAGUE

Materials:

- ☐ Template from Activity Book
- ☐ green card stock paper (or white card stock colored green)
- ☐ scissors
- ☐ craft glue
- ☐ clear tape
- ☐ googly eyes
- ☐ 2 pennies

Snack Project 1: PLAGUE FLIES DRINK

Ingredients/Materials:

- ☐ water
- ☐ ice cube tray
- ☐ mini plastic flies
- ☐ clear liquid drink such as apple juice, sprite, water, or lemonade
- ☐ clear drinking glass

Story of the Bible: The Old Testament **TEACHER'S MANUAL**

Chapter 7

Craft Project 1: PILLAR OF CLOUD AND PILLAR OF FIRE

Materials:

- ☐ 2 paper towel rolls
- ☐ craft glue
- ☐ cotton balls
- ☐ red, yellow, and orange tissue OR construction paper
- ☐ scissors

Snack Project 1: PARTING THE RED SEA CARROT MUFFIN

Ingredients:

- ☐ 1 1/3 cup all purpose flour
- ☐ 1 1/2 teaspoons baking soda
- ☐ 1 1/4 teaspoons baking powder
- ☐ 1 1/2 teaspoons cinnamon
- ☐ 1/2 teaspoon salt
- ☐ 3 eggs
- ☐ 1 cup white sugar
- ☐ 3/4 cup vegetable, canola, coconut, or other preferred baking oil
- ☐ 1 teaspoon vanilla
- ☐ 1 1/2 cups grated carrot
- ☐ 1/2 cup shredded apple
- ☐ 1/4 cup cream cheese
- ☐ 2 tablespoons softened butter
- ☐ 1 teaspoon vanilla extract
- ☐ 1 1/2 cups sifted confectioners sugar
- ☐ blue food coloring
- ☐ gummy bears

Snack Project 2: MANNA PIE CRUST

Ingredients:

- ☐ pre-made pie crust
- ☐ 1/2 cup room temperature butter
- ☐ 1/3 cup honey

Chapter 8

Craft Project 1: THE TEN COMMANDMENTS

Materials:

- ☐ Templates from Activity Book
- ☐ 4 sheets of gray or brown construction paper
- ☐ scissors
- ☐ craft glue
- ☐ clear tape

Activity Project 1: TEN COMMANDMENT DISCOVERY BAG

Materials:

1. First place ribbon, trophy, medal, or a number 1 cut out by teacher—symbolizing that God is to be first in our life

2. Small tube of toothpaste or small container of mouthwash—symbolizing that we are to keep our mouth clean by not using God's name in vain
3. Photo of Mom and Dad—symbolizing the honor due to your father and mother
4. A paper calendar with Sundays and Holy Days of Obligation circled in red—symbolizing the obligation to keep holy the Sabbath and other Holy Days
5. Plastic knife, pretend knife, or other weapon—symbolizing the precept that you should not kill
6. A heart shape broken into 2 pieces (feel free to omit as this commandment may or may not be one you have covered with your children)—symbolizing the precept forbidding adultery
7. Hand shape cut from construction paper with a piece of candy taped to the palm—symbolizing the precept forbidding theft
8. A strip of paper that says "lie, lie, lie" with each word increasing in size and in darkness (in other words, the lie grows as the further down the strip it gets)—symbolizing the precept forbidding false witness against your neighbor
9. Two rings, plastic or real—symbolizing the sacredness of marriage and the commitment involved (This will cover the ninth commandment. Here the emphasis will be on husband and wife appreciating and focusing on one another as they did the day they were married.)
10. A piece of jewelry or other pretty object that the child might see as something special—symbolizing the precept forbidding you from coveting your neighbor's goods
11. Pillowcase

Snack Project 1: TEN COMMANDMENT COOKIES

Ingredients:

- ☐ 12 tablespoons softened butter
- ☐ 2 1/2 cups powdered sugar
- ☐ 6 egg whites
- ☐ 2 tablespoons vanilla extract
- ☐ 2 teaspoons almond extract
- ☐ 1 1/2 cup flour
- ☐ 16 oz. bittersweet chocolate, chopped
- ☐ 1 cup heavy cream
- ☐ 1/2 cup unsalted butter
- ☐ freezer bag with corner cut off OR piping bag with 1/4 in. plain tip

Chapter 9

Craft Project 1: VENOMOUS SNAKE (ONE OF THE PUNISHMENTS)

Materials:

- ☐ colored construction paper
- ☐ stapler OR clear tape
- ☐ googly eyes
- ☐ craft glue
- ☐ small piece of red construction paper (for tongue)

Craft Project 2: BALAAM AND HIS DONKEY

Materials:
- ☐ Template from Activity Book
- ☐ 2 popsicle sticks
- ☐ craft glue OR clear tape
- ☐ colored pencils

Snack Project 1: TWELVE "GINGERBREAD" MEN SENT AS SPIES

Ingredients:
- ☐ 1 (3.5 ounce) package of cook-and-serve butterscotch pudding mix
- ☐ 1/2 cup of butter
- ☐ 1/2 cup packed light brown sugar
- ☐ 1 egg
- ☐ 1 1/2 cups all purpose flour
- ☐ 1/2 teaspoon baking soda
- ☐ 1 1/2 teaspoons ground ginger
- ☐ 3/4 teaspoon ground cinnamon
- ☐ 4 cups confectioners sugar
- ☐ 1/2 cup shortening
- ☐ 5 tablespoons milk
- ☐ 1 teaspoon vanilla extract
- ☐ green food coloring

Chapter 10

Craft Project 1: TRUMPET AT JERICHO

Materials:
- ☐ paper towel roll
- ☐ markers
- ☐ scissors
- ☐ 4 buttons
- ☐ hot glue gun

Craft Project 2: BUILD THE WALL OF JERICHO

Materials:
- ☐ lincoln logs, OR wooden blocks, OR Legos, OR any other building block you have
- ☐ soldier figures, OR Lego men, OR stuffed animals, OR any other figures you have to use as the army

Snack Project 1: GRAHAM CRACKER JERICHO

Ingredients:
- ☐ sandwich bread
- ☐ graham crackers
- ☐ peanut or almond butter
- ☐ gummy bears

Chapter 11

Craft Project 1: A TORCH FOR GIDEON

Materials:

- ☐ paper towel tube
- ☐ paper or styrofoam cup
- ☐ aluminum foil
- ☐ craft knife OR scissors
- ☐ red, yellow, and orange tissue OR construction paper
- ☐ craft glue

Craft Project 2: HAIR GROWING SAMSON SPOON

Materials:

- ☐ 1, 10 in. wooden craft spoon
- ☐ Template from Activity Book
- ☐ craft glue
- ☐ brown yarn
- ☐ hole punch
- ☐ 2 hole punch reinforcements (colored brown)
- ☐ markers and colored pencils.
- ☐ hot glue gun

Science Project 1: SAMSON'S GRASS HEAD

Materials:

- ☐ small plastic cup
- ☐ old pair of nylon stockings or knee-highs
- ☐ grass or alfalfa seeds
- ☐ potting soil
- ☐ googly eyes
- ☐ black felt square (or other black material)
- ☐ red felt square (or other red material)
- ☐ brown felt square (or other brown material)
- ☐ hot glue gun

Chapter 12

Craft project 1: DAVID'S MARSHMALLOW SLINGSHOT

Materials:

- ☐ 2 empty toilet paper rolls
- ☐ 2 large rubber bands (do not need to be thick, but do need to be at least 2 in. in diameter)
- ☐ pencil
- ☐ strong tape (such as duct tape)
- ☐ hole punch reinforcements
- ☐ mini marshmallows

Story of the Bible: The Old Testament **TEACHER'S MANUAL**

Craft Project 2: TOILET PAPER ROLL DAVID AND PAPER TOWEL ROLL GOLIATH

Materials:
- ☐ Templates from Activity Book
- ☐ coloring pencils
- ☐ craft glue
- ☐ scissors

Chapter 13

Craft Project 1: MAKE A CROWN FOR KING DAVID
(Save for use in Chapter 14)

Materials:
- ☐ gold poster board
- ☐ stapler
- ☐ craft gems OR markers
- ☐ craft glue OR hot glue gun

Chapter 14

Activity 1: ACT OUT KING SOLOMON AND THE TWO MOTHERS

Supplies:
- ☐ crown from Chapter 13 Activity
- ☐ baby doll or stuffed animal
- ☐ three actors/actresses

Chapter 16

Craft Project 1: PAPER PLATE RAVEN

Materials:
- ☐ 3 paper plates
- ☐ black marker
- ☐ scissors
- ☐ stapler
- ☐ googly eyes
- ☐ yellow construction paper
- ☐ metal round paper fasteners

Activity Materials at a Glance

Craft project 2: ALTAR AT BAAL PROVING GOD IS THE ONE TRUE GOD

Materials:

- ☐ white construction paper
- ☐ brown construction paper
- ☐ blue marker
- ☐ craft glue
- ☐ orange and yellow tissue OR construction paper
- ☐ craft or popsicle sticks cut into 3 inch segments.

Snack Project 1: THE RAVEN BRINGS BREAD AND MEAT

Ingredients:

- ☐ bread (any type desired)
- ☐ deli meat (any type desired)

Chapter 17

Snack Project 1: CANDY TRIALS OF JOB

Ingredient:

- ☐ bag of candy-coated chocolates

Craft Project 1: STYROFOAM CUP WHALE

Materials:

- ☐ styrofoam cup
- ☐ blue paint
- ☐ silver OR white pipe cleaner
- ☐ googly eyes
- ☐ blue construction paper
- ☐ red construction paper
- ☐ stapler
- ☐ craft glue OR hot glue gun
- ☐ Lego figure or other small "man" figure

Snack Project 2: GOLDFISH CRACKERS

Ingredient:

- ☐ Goldfish crackers

Science Project 1: SATAN TRIES TO PULL JOB IN

Materials:

- ☐ glass Erlenmeyer flask OR glass bottle with the opening smaller than body of the bottle
- ☐ water balloon
- ☐ water
- ☐ match
- ☐ scrap of paper

Chapter 18

Craft Project: JUDITH'S SWORD

Materials:

- ☐ empty wrapping paper tube
- ☐ 9 in. by 3 in. strip of cardboard
- ☐ aluminum foil
- ☐ scissors
- ☐ markers
- ☐ craft jewels (if desired)
- ☐ hot glue (if using craft jewels)

Chapter 19

Craft Project 1: FIERY FURNACE PAPER BAG

Materials:

- ☐ Templates from Activity Book
- ☐ popsicle sticks OR straws
- ☐ colored pencils
- ☐ paper lunch bag
- ☐ clear tape

Craft Project 2: DANIEL AND THE LION WOODEN SPOONS

Materials:

- ☐ 2, 10 in. wooden spoons
- ☐ Templates from Activity Book
- ☐ small piece of scrap fabric (preferably a neutral color)
- ☐ brown yarn
- ☐ markers
- ☐ colored pencils
- ☐ hot glue gun

Snack Project 1: FIERY FURNACE S'MORES

Ingredients:

- ☐ graham cracker squares
- ☐ regular size marshmallows
- ☐ mini chocolate bars
- ☐ little bear graham crackers
- ☐ aluminum foil

Chapter 20

Craft Project 1: A RAM'S HORN

Materials:

- ☐ party blower
- ☐ brown construction paper
- ☐ brown yarn
- ☐ brown marker
- ☐ rubber band
- ☐ stapler
- ☐ hole punch
- ☐ hole punch reinforcements

Chapter 21

Craft Project 1: A CROWN FOR QUEEN ESTHER

Materials:

- ☐ poster board in desired colored
- ☐ stapler
- ☐ craft gems OR markers
- ☐ craft glue OR hot glue gun
  (You may find that hot glue allows for more vigorous play.)

Craft Project 2: A ROYAL SCEPTER FOR QUEEN ESTHER

Materials:

- ☐ 1, 3 in. polystyrene ball
- ☐ 1, 12 in. thin dowel
- ☐ aluminum foil
- ☐ craft gems
- ☐ hot glue gun
- ☐ non-washable markers in desired colors

Chapter 22

Craft Project 1: TREASURE CHEST

Materials:

- ☐ shoe box
- ☐ yellow construction paper
- ☐ black construction paper
- ☐ craft glue
- ☐ gold-covered chocolate coins
- ☐ any leftover craft gems from other projects
- ☐ black marker

INTRODUCTION
Your Time Has Come

LISTENING TO GOD'S WORD
Psalm 119:105
> Thy word is a lamp to my feet
> and a light to my path.

QUESTIONS FOR REVIEW

1. **What can we learn about God from the Book of Nature?**

   We can learn many things about God from the "Book of Nature." For example, we can learn that God is beautiful, powerful, loving, and caring.

2. **Name three reasons why the "Book of Nature" cannot tell us all that we need to know about God.**

   We aren't always able to read correctly the wonderful lessons that are found in the "Book of Nature." The things of this world are so beautiful and powerful and good that we may be tempted to think more of them than we do of the God who made them. Many important things about God aren't written in the "Book of Nature" because they are above and beyond nature; they are supernatural.

3. **How can we trust that everything God says is true? What do we call the truths that we cannot fully understand?**

   We can trust God because He knows all things and cannot lie. The truths that we can't fully understand, even after God has told them to us, we call mysteries.

4. **What do we call the help that God gave the sacred writers of the Bible?**

   divine inspiration

5. **What does the Old Testament tell us about?**

    It tells us about the covenant between God and His people before Jesus came into the world.

6. **What does the New Testament tell us about?**

    The New Testament tells us how God's Promise was fulfilled in Jesus Christ and His Church.

7. **Define Sacred Scripture and Sacred Tradition.**

    Sacred Scripture is the Bible.

    Sacred Tradition encompasses truths about our faith that were not written down in the Bible but have come to us by word of mouth and by example, beginning with the apostles.

NARRATION EXERCISES

Book of Nature

We can learn many things about God from the Book of Nature. By looking at His creation we can tell that God is beautiful, powerful, loving, and caring.

Scared Scripture and Sacred Tradition

Scared Scripture is the Bible, which is made up of the Old and New Testaments. Sacred Tradition is comprised of the truths that we have learned through examples and that have been passed down orally.

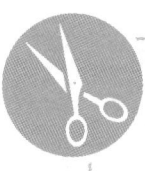

CRAFT PROJECT

Book of Nature

(Activity Book Pages 5–8)

Remove and color pages 5–8 in the activity book. Fold the pages so as to make your own "Book of Nature." Staple in two places on the fold line to bind the book.

PART ONE
How God Came to Promise Us a Redeemer

CHAPTER 1
In the Beginning

LISTENING TO GOD'S WORD

Genesis 1:27

So God created man in his own image, in the image of God he created him; male and female he created them.

QUESTIONS FOR REVIEW

1. How and why did God create heaven and earth?

   He made them out of nothing not because He needed them but so that creatures could share in His happiness and glory.

2. What do we learn from the Book of Genesis?

   We can learn how God made the world.

3. In what order did God create the things of the world?

   light
   heaven
   earth and sea
   sun, moon, and stars
   fish and birds
   beasts and man

4. How did God make man, and what did he give man dominion over?

   God made man in His own image from the dust of the earth and breathed into him the breath of life. God gave man dominion over the fish of the sea, the birds of the air, the cattle, all the earth, and over every creeping thing that creeps upon the earth.

5. What do the names "Adam" and "Eve" mean?

   Adam: Earthborn
   Eve: Mother of all the living

6. Satan appeared to Eve in what form? What did he tell Eve in order to deceive her?

   Satan appeared as a serpent and deceived Eve by telling her that God had lied to them and that the fruit would not cause their death but would make them like God.

7. What do we call this first sin? What was the punishment for eating of the forbidden fruit?

   We call this first sin original sin. Adam and Eve were cast out of the garden and told that "you are dust, and to dust you shall return."

8. Why do all generations after Adam and Eve lack original righteousness?

   They lack original righteousness because Adam and Eve could not pass on that which they no longer possessed.

NARRATION EXERCISES

Creation

God created heaven and earth and all that is in it. God made man from the dust of the earth and gave him dominion over all the earth.

Adam and Eve

The first man was Adam and the first woman was Eve. God made them in his image. God gave them free will. Satan tricked Eve into eating the fruit of the forbidden tree and she gave the fruit to Adam who ate as well. As punishment they were sent from the Garden of Eden and would bear the consequences of death and suffering.

Activity Projects

COLORING PAGE

Adam, Eve, and the Snake *(Activity Book Page 9)*

Color the picture of Adam and Eve being tricked by the snake.

CHAPTER 1: **In the Beginning**

WORD SEARCH

Adam and Eve: *(Activity Book Pages 11–12)*

Fill in the blanks for the Adam and Eve word search clues and then find the corresponding words in the word search. Note: There is a word bank at the end of the word search to aid the student.

Word Search Answer Key:

1. Adam
2. earthborn
3. Eden
4. knowledge
5. beasts
6. birds
7. name
8. alone
9. ribs
10. bone
11. flesh
12. woman
13. Eve
14. mother
15. grace
16. serve
17. Satan
18. envied
19. serpent
20. die
21. trick
22. ate
23. fruit
24. disobey
26. hide
26. God

CRAFT PROJECT 1: PAPER PLATE SNAKE WIND TWIRLER

Materials:
☐ paper plate
☐ any color washable paint for your snake
☐ hot glue gun
☐ red yarn
☐ craft googly eyes
☐ scissors

Directions:
1. Paint both sides of your paper plate any color you want the body of your snake to be.
2. Use a pencil to draw a spiral beginning at the outside of the plate and circling your way inward (rings should be 1 to 1 1/2 in. thick).
3. Hot glue the googly eyes on the center circle of the paper plate.
4. Use scissors to cut along the circular lines being sure to leave a small circular area in the middle of your plate.
5. Use the hot glue gun to adhere the red yarn to your plate.
6. Holding the yarn, run with your snake behind you and watch as it twirls in the wind.

CRAFT PROJECT 2: MAKE THE TREE OF KNOWLEDGE

Materials:

- ☐ empty toilet paper roll
- ☐ 6 in. cardboard square
- ☐ brown pipe cleaner
- ☐ brown and green craft
- ☐ paint brush
- ☐ red craft beads
- ☐ hot glue gun
- ☐ hole punch

Directions:

1. Paint the toilet paper roll brown.
2. Paint the 6 in. cardboard square green.
3. Punch 6 holes, evenly spaced, at the top of the tree trunk.
4. Thread the brown pipe cleaner through the holes (use 2 pipe cleaners in each hole). They should cross the center of the toilet paper roll and go out the opposite hole. Bend and twist the pipe cleaner into branches.
5. Cut 24 small leaves (tear shaped) from the green construction paper and hole punch each one. Thread some of the leaves onto the pipe cleaner.
6. Now thread some of the red craft beads onto the pipe cleaner (these are apples).
7. Finish off by placing the remaining leaves on the pipe cleaner and securing the ends by twisting the pipe cleaner through and around the remaining red beads.
8. Enjoy!

SNACK PROJECT 1: THIRD DAY OF CREATION SNACK

"And God said, 'Let the waters under the heavens be gathered together into one place, and let the dry land appear.' And God said, 'Let the earth put forth vegetation, plants yielding seed, and fruit trees bearing fruit in which is their seed, each according to its kind, upon the earth.' And it was so. And God saw that it was good. And there was evening and there was morning, a third day."

Ingredients:

- ☐ 6 cups of crispy rice cereal
- ☐ 1 (10 ounce) package of regular marshmallows OR 4 cups of mini marshmallows
- ☐ 3 tablespoons butter
- ☐ green food coloring
- ☐ blue food coloring
- ☐ any fruit you want (the more visible the seed the better)
- ☐ any variety of vegetable

Directions:

1. In a large saucepan, melt the butter over low heat. Add in the marshmallows and stir until melted completely. Remove the pan from the heat.

2. Mix in the crispy rice cereal and stir until evenly coated.
3. Divide the batch into two portions.
4. Add blue food coloring to 1/2 of the mixture and green food coloring to the other 1/2 of the mixture.
5. Allow your mixture to cool slightly so that it isn't too hot to handle.
6. Add the blue and green together in chunks to create the "earth." There should be at least one clearly defined "continent."
7. Serve your crispy rice "earth" treat alongside your favorite fruits and vegetables.
8. Now you have the dry land gathered and separated by the seas and the vegetation that God created.
9. Enjoy!

SNACK PROJECT 2: GARDEN OF EDEN PIZZA PIE

Ingerdients:
- ☐ 1 1/4 cup white sugar
- ☐ 1 cup butter
- ☐ 3 egg yolks
- ☐ 1 teaspoon vanilla extract
- ☐ 2 1/2 cups all-purpose flour
- ☐ 1 teaspoon baking soda
- ☐ 1/2 teaspoon cream of tartar
- ☐ 1 (8 ounce) package of cream cheese, softened
- ☐ 1 (8 ounce) container of frozen whipped topping (thaw)
- ☐ dash of salt
- ☐ 1 tablespoon cornstarch
- ☐ 1/2 cup of orange juice
- ☐ 2 tablespoons lemon juice
- ☐ 1/4 cup water
- ☐ 1/2 teaspoon orange zest
- ☐ strawberries
- ☐ kiwi
- ☐ bananas
- ☐ blueberries
- ☐ mandarin slices

Directions:
1. Preheat oven to 350 degrees F.
2. Grease a glass pie pan.
3. Cream together sugar and butter.
4. Beat in egg yolks and vanilla.
5. Add flour, baking soda, and cream of tarter and combine.
6. Press dough evenly into pie plate. You want the crust to be 1/4–1/2 in. thick. Refrigerate any left-over dough.
7. Bake in preheated oven for approximately 10–12 minutes. Keep an eye out as cooking times may vary.

8. In a large bowl, combine softened cream cheese and whipped topping (already thawed).
9. Spread cream cheese mixture over cooled pie crust.
10. Cut all fruit into flat pieces as a topping for the pie. If you use bananas, coat them with lemon juice to prevent browning.
11. Arrange strawberries, kiwi, bananas, blueberries, mandarins, and any other desired fruits over the topping. A circular pattern working from the outside in with a new fruit for each ring makes a pretty presentation.
12. Chill while you prepare the glaze.
13. In a medium saucepan, combine sugar, salt, cornstarch, orange juice, lemon juice, and water.
14. Place over medium heat and bring to a boil. Continue to cook 1–2 minutes or until it begins to thicken.
15. Remove from heat and add in orange zest.
16. Cool slightly, do not allow it to begin to set up.
17. Spoon over the fruit.
18. Chill pie for around 2 hours or until it has firmed enough to cut into slices.
19. Enjoy!

SCIENCE PROJECT 1: SECOND DAY OF CREATION LAVA LAMP

"Let there be a firmament in the midst of the waters, and let it separate the waters from the waters."

Materials:
- ☐ wax paper OR plastic funnel
- ☐ vegetable oil OR canola oil
- ☐ blue food coloring
- ☐ 3/4 cup water
- ☐ Alka-Seltzer tablets
- ☐ 2 liter plastic bottle with lid (soda bottle)

This experiment can also be done on a smaller scale with a clear plastic water bottle.

Directions:
1. Use wax paper to make a homemade funnel if needed.
2. Place funnel into top of 2 liter plastic bottle.

3. Pour 3/4 cup water into the bottle.
4. Fill the remainder of the bottle with vegetable or canola oil.
5. Wait for the water and oil to separate.
6. Add 10 drops of food coloring into the bottle.
7. Wait for food coloring to make its way through the oil and into the water at the bottom. Lightly swirl to fully mix food coloring into water.
8. Break an Alka-Seltzer tablet in half and drop into bottle.
9. Continue to keep the lava lamp going by adding more Alka-Seltzer tablets as the lamp slows down.
10. Enjoy!

CHAPTER 2
Descendants of Adam and Eve

LISTENING TO GOD'S WORD
Genesis 9:1
And God blessed Noah and his sons, and said to them, "Be fruitful and multiply, and fill the earth."

QUESTIONS FOR REVIEW

1. **Why did Adam and Eve's descendants have cause to hope despite the effect of original sin?**

   They had cause to hope because God had promised that a descendant of Eve would crush the serpent's head.

2. **Why was God displeased with Cain's sacrifice?**

   Cain did not give his offering with a pure heart and this was displeasing to God.

3. **In the story of Noah, how did God destroy the earth?**

   He destroyed the earth by a great flood.

4. **How did Noah track when the waters had gone down?**

   He sent out a dove.

5. **What was the name of the giant tower that was never completed, and why wasn't it finished?**

   It was called the tower of Babel, which means confusion. It was never completed because God knew that the men who were building it were proud in their hearts and worked for their own selfish glory. God stopped the project by making it so that they could not understand one another; hence the name denoting confusion.

6. Name 3 of the lands where great nations eventually formed.
   Egypt
   Mesopotamia
   Canaan

NARRATION EXERCISES

Cain and Abel

Cain and Abel were the sons of Adam and Eve. Cain grew very jealous of Abel and killed him. God punished Cain by condemning him to wander the earth in exile. God put a mark on Cain so that others would know not to kill him. We see in Cain the effect of his parents' sin.

Noah

Because of man's wickedness, God destroyed the earth with a great flood. Noah and his family were righteous and were spared. Noah built a great ark so that the goodness of creation would be saved. He did as God commanded and took two of every kind of animal. It rained for forty days and forty nights. Noah sent out a dove to check if the waters were going down. When the dove returned with an olive branch Noah knew the waters were going down. God promised to never again destroy the earth with the waters of a flood.

MAP ACTIVITY: TOWER OF BABEL

(Activity Book Page 17)

1. Find the Tigris and Euphrates Rivers.
2. Look at the land between these two rivers. The land in the central southern part of this region would be what is referred to as Shinar.
3. Locate the narrow strip of land where the Tigris and Euphrates Rivers run close together. We will approximate that this region is where the tower of Babel may have been built.
4. Draw your own tower of Babel in this area and label this area "Shinar."

CHAPTER 2: **Descendants of Adam and Eve**

Activity Projects

COLORING PAGES

Cain and Abel *(Activity Book Page 13)*
Color the picture of Cain killing Abel.

Tower of Babel *(Activity Book Page 15)*
Color the picture of the Tower of Babel.

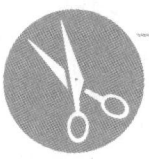

CRAFT PROJECT 1: NOAH'S ARK

(Activity Book Pages 21–23)

Materials:
- ☐ activity page from Activity Book
- ☐ scissors
- ☐ glue
- ☐ markers
- ☐ clear tape

Directions:
1. Cut out pieces from activity page. Do not cut along the dotted lines.
2. Color the pieces in any way you want.
3. Fold the boat along the dotted line.
4. Bring up the bow of the ark and use clear tape to tape together. Repeat procedure with the stern.
5. Fold the "cabin" along the dotted lines and tape together at the bottom.
6. Use a glue stick to adhere the cabin to the center of the boat.
7. Enjoy!

CRAFT PROJECT 2: CAIN THE FARMER AND ABEL THE SHEPHERD SPOON PEOPLE

(Activity Book Pages 25–27)

Materials:
- ☐ 2, 10 in. wooden spoons
- ☐ brown pipe cleaner
- ☐ scissors
- ☐ small piece of scrap fabric (preferably a neutral color)
- ☐ markers
- ☐ colored pencils
- ☐ hot glue gun
- ☐ Template from Activity Book

Directions:

1. Cut out and color Abel's body from the Activity Book. Hot glue his body onto the spoon.
2. Cut a small scrap of fabric and fashion over top of Abel's head. Hot glue into place.
3. Cut pipe cleaner in half. Bend one half for shepherd's crook and glue onto Abel's body. Use the other half of the pipe cleaner to wrap around the shepherd's hat.
4. Use markers to add eyes, a nose, and a mouth to Abel.
5. Cut out and color Cain's body from the Activity Book. Hot glue his body onto the spoon.
6. Color the fruit bowl. Use colored pencils to add in any fruits or vegetables you want.
7. Cut the fruit bowl out and glue to Cain's hand.
8. Use markers to add hair, eyes, a nose, and a mouth to Cain.
9. Enjoy!

SCIENCE PROJECT 1: CAIN'S AND ABEL'S HEARTS

Materials:
- ☐ 2 clear glasses
- ☐ water
- ☐ white vinegar
- ☐ green food coloring
- ☐ baking soda

Directions:

1. Fill one glass 1/3 of the way full with water. This represents Abel's pure heart.
2. Fill the next glass 1/3 of the way full with vinegar.
3. Add a couple of drops of green food coloring into the vinegar glass. This represents Cain's jealous heart.
4. Add one teaspoon of baking soda to the cup with water. This represents Abel's pure gift to God. Notice that Abel's heart remains calm and clear.
5. Add one teaspoon of baking soda to the cup with vinegar. This represents Cain giving his gift to God with an impure heart. Notice how Cain's heart boils and bubbles over. This is what jealousy, anger, and resentment do in our hearts.
6. Enjoy!

CHAPTER 2: **Descendants of Adam and Eve**

SNACK PROJECT 1: NOAH'S BANANA ARK

Ingredients:
- ☐ banana
- ☐ peanut butter
- ☐ animal crackers

Directions:
1. Place banana in a bowl and split in half lengthwise.
2. Add peanut butter to the center of the banana "ark."
3. Place animal crackers in the middle of the peanut butter.
4. Enjoy!

CROSSWORD PUZZLE: NOAH'S ARK

(Activity Book Page 19)

Across:
2. Flood
4. Grapes
6. Ham
7. Mountain
9. Ark
10. Olive

Down:
1. Dove
2. Faithful
3. Animal
5. Rainbow
8. Three

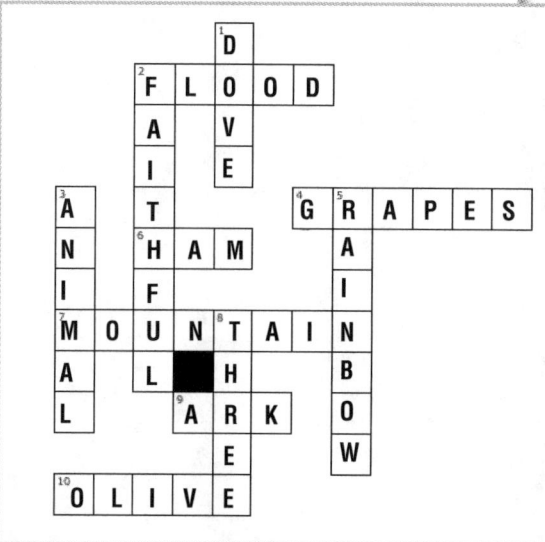

PART TWO
How God Founded the Nation From Which the Redeemer of the World Came

CHAPTER 3
Abraham and Isaac

LISTENING TO GOD'S WORD

Genesis 15:1

After these things the word of the Lord came to Abram in a vision, "Fear not, Abram, I am your shield; your reward shall be very great."

QUESTIONS FOR REVIEW

1. **What did God promise to Abram even though he and Sarai had no children?**
   God promised that he would be the father of a great nation.

2. **Where did God command Abram to go?**
   Abram was commanded to go to the land of Canaan.

3. **What news did the guests at Abraham's tent share with him?**
   They shared the news that Sarah would soon have a son.

4. **What did God say would happen to the cities of Sodom and Gomorrah? What was Abraham's response?**
   God said he would destroy the cities because of the sinfulness of the people. Abraham bargained with God striking an agreement that the cities would be saved if only ten righteous men were found living there.

5. **What happened to the cities? Was anyone saved?**
   Two angels were sent by God to destroy the cities. They warned Lot to leave with his loved ones.

6. **What happened to Lot's wife?**

    Despite the angel's warning not to look back, Lot's wife was curious and turned back to see. She was instantly turned into a pillar of salt.

7. **What did God ask as a sacrifice from Abraham? Why did He ask for this most precious thing?**

    God asked Abraham to sacrifice his beloved son Isaac. He did this to test Abraham's obedience and faith.

8. **How did God help Abraham's servant find the right wife for Isaac? Who was this woman?**

    God said that he was to choose the woman who offered both him and his camels a drink at the well. Rebecca did this and the servant was overjoyed.

NARRATION EXERCISES

Abraham

God promised Abraham that he would be the father of a great nation. He sent Abraham to Canaan. Abraham was a righteous man who found favor with God.

Abraham's Sacrifice

Abraham so loved God and trusted in Him that he was willing to sacrifice even his most beloved son Isaac. He took Isaac to the mountain that God had commanded and built an altar. He tied up Isaac and was ready to kill him when God stopped him and said that he should not harm Isaac. Abraham had passed God's test.

MAP ACTIVITY: GOD CALLS ABRAHAM

(Activity Book Page 33)

1. Locate Ur on your map. This is the city that Abram lived in with his wife, Sarai, and his father, Terah. Circle Ur in blue.
2. With a blue colored pencil, draw a line from Ur up to Haran. This is where Terah moved the family. Abram moved with his father.

3. After the death of Terah, God told Abram to move his family to the land he would show him, the land of Canaan. With a yellow colored pencil, draw a line from Haran to the land of Canaan. This is the land to which God brought Abraham.

Activity Projects

COLORING PAGES

Abraham and Isaac *(Activity Book Page 29)*

Color the picture of Abraham and Isaac.

CRAFT PROJECT 1: A TENT FOR ABRAM AND SARAI

Materials:
- ☐ 4–6 twigs, each 10–12 inches in length
- ☐ 2 rubber bands
- ☐ 24 in. square of brown fabric
- ☐ scissors

Directions:
1. Collect 4–6 twigs that are 10–12 inches in length.
2. Use a rubber band to secure the twigs at one end. This will be the frame for the tent.
3. Cut brown fabric in a 24 in. square. Make a small circular hole in the middle of the square.
4. Put the top of the twigs through the opening in the fabric. Secure with a second rubber band if desired.
5. Cut an opening for the tent.
6. Enjoy!

CRAFT PROJECT 2: STARS IN THE SKY

Materials:
- ☐ 24 oz. or larger glass jar (pickle jar works great)
- ☐ piece of aluminum foil
- ☐ nail
- ☐ battery-operated tea light candle

Directions:
1. Thoroughly clean and dry out the jar.
2. Cut a piece of aluminum foil to line the interior of your jar.
3. Use the nail to punch holes of various sizes all over the piece of aluminum foil. You want TONS of holes.
4. Line the inside of your jar with the foil.
5. Place the battery-operated tea light in the middle of your jar.
6. Go into a dark closet and enjoy your stars in the sky. This craft works well as a night-light too.
7. Enjoy!

CRAFT PROJECT 3: A RAM FOR THE SACRIFICE

(Activity Book Page 31)

Materials:
- ☐ Template from the Activity Book
- ☐ cotton balls
- ☐ craft glue
- ☐ coloring pencils
- ☐ scissors

Directions:
1. Color the horns, face, and legs of the ram.
2. Cut the ram out.
3. Glue the cotton balls all over the body of the ram.
4. Enjoy!

CHAPTER 4
Jacob, the Son of Isaac

LISTENING TO GOD'S WORD
Genesis 28:10-14

Jacob left Beer-sheba, and went toward Haran. And he came to a certain place, and stayed there that night, because the sun had set. Taking one of the stones of the place, he put it under his head and lay down in that place to sleep. And he dreamed that there was a ladder set up on the earth, and the top of it reached to heaven; and behold, the angels of God were ascending and descending on it! And behold, the Lord stood above it and said, "I am the Lord, the God of Abraham your father and the God of Isaac; the land on which you lie I will give to you and to your descendants; and your descendants shall be like the dust of the earth, and you shall spread abroad to the west and to the east and to the north and to the south; and by you and your descendants shall all the families of the earth bless themselves."

QUESTIONS FOR REVIEW

1. **What did it mean to receive the birthright?**

   It meant receiving a larger portion of the wealth, becoming the head and priest of the family, and obtaining a special blessing before the death of one's father.

2. **How did Jacob and Rebecca deceive Isaac?**

   Jacob delivered Isaac's stew with his neck and hands covered in animal skins so that he would seem hairy like his brother Esau.

3. **How did Esau respond to Jacob receiving the birthright? How did Esau change over time?**

   He was furious and vowed to kill Jacob. Over time, Esau came to forgive Jacob and welcomed him back.

4. **How was Jacob deceived?**

   He was lied to by Laban and had to marry Laban's oldest daughter Leah as well as Rachel.

5. **What did Jacob dream about at Bethel? What did God promise him?**

   Jacob dreamed about angels ascending and descending between heaven and earth. God promised to give him and his descendants the land where he was sleeping.

NARRATION EXERCISES

Jacob and the Birthright

Jacob and his mother, Rebecca, deceived Isaac into giving the birthright to Jacob instead of his older brother Esau. They did this by cooking the food Isaac had requested and covering Jacob with animal skins so that he would feel hairy like his brother Esau.

MAP ACTIVITY: JACOB LEAVES CANAAN

(Activity Book Page 43)

1. After he had stolen Esau's birthright, Rebecca told Jacob to flee Canaan and to go to the land of Haran. Draw a red line from Canaan to Haran.
2. At Bethel, draw a golden ladder symbolizing the dream Jacob had along the way.
3. At Haran, draw a pair of yellow rings intertwined symbolizing that this is where Jacob was married.
4. Using a red pencil, draw a return route for Jacob and his family from Haran to Shechem, which is in the land of Canaan.
5. Now continue in red to Bethel where God sent Jacob. Draw an altar here as Jacob built an altar and offered sacrifice to God.
6. From Bethel, continue in red to Bethlehem.
7. From Bethlehem continue in red to Hebron where Jacob went to be with his father Isaac.

CHAPTER 4 : **Jacob, the Son of Isaac**

Activity Projects

COLORING PAGES

Jacob's Dream *(Activity Book Page 35)*
  Color the picture of Jacob's Dream.

Esau *(Activity Book Page 37)*
  Color the picture of the hairy Esau.

SNACK PROJECT 1: JACOB AND ESAU HAM AND POTATO SOUP

(8 servings)

Ingredients:
- ☐ 4 cups diced potatoes
- ☐ 1/2 cup chopped celery
- ☐ 1 cup diced cooked ham
- ☐ 3 1/4 cups water
- ☐ 2 tablespoons chicken bouillon
- ☐ 6 tablespoons butter or margarine
- ☐ salt to taste
- ☐ pepper to taste
- ☐ 6 tablespoons all purpose flour
- ☐ 2 1/3 cups of milk
- ☐ green onions to garnish

Directions:
1. Combine potatoes, celery, ham, and water in a large stockpot.
2. Bring to a boil and cook over medium heat for about 15 minutes until the potatoes are tender and a fork easily slips in and out of the potato.
3. Stir in the chicken bouillon, salt, and pepper.
4. In a second saucepan, melt butter over medium-low heat and then whisk in flour with a fork. Stir continuously until thick. Slowly add in milk watching that lumps do not form until all the milk is added. Continue to stir over medium-low heat for about 5 minutes or until thick.
5. Stir milk mixture into the stockpot with potato mixture and heat thoroughly.
6. Serve in bowl garnished with green onion.
7. Enjoy!

SNACK PROJECT 2: JACOB'S LADDER

Ingredients:
- ☐ pretzel sticks
- ☐ mini marshmallows

Directions:
1. Connect the pretzels and marshmallows to form a ladder.
2. See how long you can make it, the longer the better!
3. Enjoy!

CRAFT PROJECT 1: JACOB AND ESAU SPOON PEOPLE

(Activity Book Page 39–41)

Materials:
- ☐ 2, 10 in. wooden craft spoons
- ☐ Templates from Activity Book
- ☐ hot glue gun
- ☐ craft glue
- ☐ brown yarn
- ☐ markers

Directions:
1. Cut out and color Jacob and Esau's bodies from the Activity Book and hot glue them onto the spoons.
2. Cut 2, 12 in. pieces of brown yarn. Loop one piece at a time into several loops and then hot glue onto spoons as beards for Jacob and Esau.
3. Cut 8, 2 in. pieces of brown yarn. Glue 4 onto each side of Jacob's body (where arms would be, this is his furry covering for tricking Isaac).
4. Cut a small soup bowl for Esau and use craft glue to attach it to Esau's body (this is the soup for which he sold his birthright).
5. Cut a small piece of paper and label "birthright." Use craft glue to attach it to Jacob.
6. Use markers to draw on hair, eyes, a nose, and a mouth for both spoon figures.
7. Enjoy!

CHAPTER 5
Joseph, the Son of Jacob

LISTENING TO GOD'S WORD

Genesis 50:19-20

But Joseph said to them, "Fear not, for am I in the place of God? As for you, you meant evil against me; but God meant it for good, to bring it about that many people should be kept alive, as they are today."

QUESTIONS FOR REVIEW

1. **Give three reasons why Joseph's brothers did not like him.**
    1. Joseph saw them doing wrong and reported it to their father.
    2. Joseph was shown special favor by their father and the brothers were jealous.
    3. Joseph shared his dreams with them, which indicated that he would one day rule over them.

2. **How did Joseph come to live in Egypt?**
   His brothers sold him as a slave to some merchants who took him to Egypt.

3. **Name some positions Joseph held in Egypt.**
   - head of Potiphar's household
   - head of the prisoners where he was jailed
   - governor of Egypt as appointed by Pharaoh

4. **How did Joseph get out of prison?**
   He was summoned by the pharaoh to interpret his dreams.

5. **What did the dream about the seven cows mean? What did Joseph advise pharaoh to do?**

   The seven fat cows were seven years of plenty in which Egypt would enjoy abundance. The seven skinny cows were seven years of famine that would follow the years of abundance. Joseph said that Pharaoh should appoint a very wise man to store away one fifth of all the grain raised during the seven fruitful years so that when the famine came there would be enough food saved up for everyone.

6. **Why did Joseph's brothers come to Egypt, and how did Joseph react?**

   Joseph's brothers came to Egypt because famine had come to Canaan and they heard that Egypt had grain. Joseph tested them by pretending not to believe them. He threw them in jail for three days and asked them to produce their youngest brother as proof of their truthfulness.

7. **What did Joseph have his servant hide in Benjamin's sack of grain? Why?**

   Joseph had his own silver chalice hidden in the sack. He was once again testing his brothers. When he saw that Judah was ready to give his life for Benjamin he could bear it no longer and told his brothers who he really was.

NARRATION EXERCISES

Joseph

Joseph's brothers did not like him. Joseph told on his brothers when he saw them doing bad things. Joseph was also their father's favorite and this made his brothers jealous. Joseph had dreams that indicated he would one-day rule over his brothers and this made his brothers angry. One day Joseph's brothers threw him into a pit and then sold him into slavery. He was taken to Egypt where he became the head of a great house. The wife of his employer lied about him and Joseph was thrown in prison. Joseph interpreted the dreams of a baker and a butler. His interpretations came true. Later, the butler remembered Joseph's ability and told the pharaoh who sent for Joseph. When Joseph interpreted the pharaoh's dream, the pharaoh made Joseph second in command. Joseph was in charge of storing up food during the good years to prepare for the coming famine. When the famine hit Canaan, Joseph's brothers came to see if they could buy food. They did not recognize Joseph, but he knew them. He tested them to see if they had changed. They had. Joseph forgave his brothers.

CHAPTER 5: **Joseph, the Son of Jacob**

MAP ACTIVITY: JOSEPH IS SOLD INTO SLAVERY

(Activity Book Page 55)

1. Locate the land of Canaan where Jacob and his sons lived. Draw a coat of many colors here symbolizing both Jacob's favor toward Joseph and Joseph's brothers' jealousy towards him.
2. Draw also a few coins showing that this is where his brothers sold Joseph into slavery.
3. Draw a red line from the land of Canaan to the land of Egypt.
4. In Egypt, draw a ring with the number 2 inside it showing that Joseph eventually became second in command in Egypt and that pharaoh gave him his ring, fine robes, and many riches.

Activity Projects

COLORING PAGES

Joseph's Torn Coat *(Activity Book Page 45)*
Color the picture of Jacob's sorrow at the sight of his son Joseph's torn and bloody coat.

Joseph and His Brothers *(Activity Book Page 47)*
Color the picture of Joseph surrounded by his brothers just as his dream had predicted he would be.

CROSSWORD PUZZLE

Joseph *(Activity Page 49)*

Down:
1. Reuben
2. Grain
5. Famine
7. Potiphar
8. Resentment
9. Dreams

Across:
3. Jealous
4. Blood
6. Benjamin
10. Governor
11. Canaan
12. Slave
13. Egypt
14. Coat

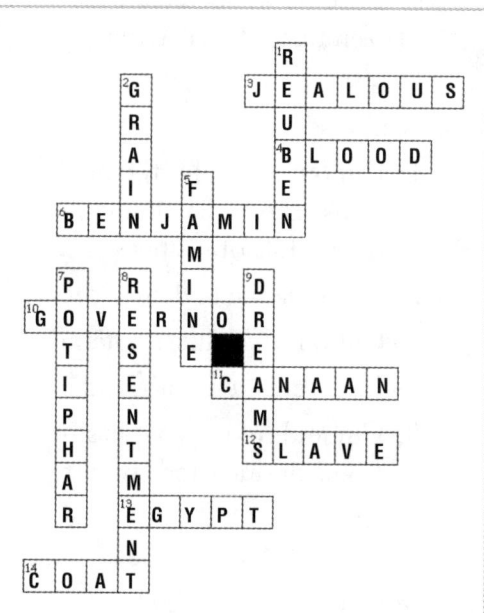

CRAFT PROJECT 1: JOSEPH'S COAT OF MANY COLORS

Materials:
- ☐ several colors of construction paper
- ☐ paper grocery bag
- ☐ scissors
- ☐ craft glue
- ☐ clear tape (for reinforcement if desired)

Directions:
1. Cut armholes and a head hole in your brown paper grocery bag.
2. Cut open the front of your vest beginning at the bottom and working your way toward the head hole.
3. Cut 1 in. thick strips of construction paper (strips should be 1" x 11").
4. Glue strips in alternating colors onto the paper bag.
5. Use tape to reinforce tops and bottoms of strips if desired.
6. Enjoy!

CRAFT PROJECT 2: THE BUTLER AND THE BAKER SPOON PEOPLE

(Activity Book Page 51–53)

Note: These spoon people are clearly not what a butler and baker would have looked like in the time of Joseph; they are, however, a fun representation for the kids.

Materials:
- ☐ 2, 10 in. wooden craft spoons
- ☐ Templates from Activity Book
- ☐ coloring pencils
- ☐ hot glue gun
- ☐ scissors

Directions:
1. Cut out and color the bodies of the butler and the baker from the Activity Book. The butler should have black suit and tie, and a white rectangle in the middle of his body. The baker can be any color.
2. Hot glue the bodies of the butler and baker to the wooden spoons.
3. Cut out the baker's hat and glue it to the top of the spoon.
4. Draw eyes, a mouth, and a nose on both spoons.
5. Cut and color a couple small pastries from the template in the Activity Book, or draw and cut out your own! Glue them onto the baker.
6. Enjoy!

SNACK PROJECT 1: SACK OF GRAIN-OLA

Ingredients:
- 4 cups rolled oats
- 3/4 cup oat bran
- 3/4 cup ground flax seed
- 1/2 cup sunflower or pumpkin seeds
- 3/4 cup finely chopped pecans
- 3/4 cup finely chopped walnuts
- 1/4 cup brown sugar
- 1/4 cup and 2 tablespoons honey
- 3/4 teaspoon salt
- 1/2 cup oil (you can use vegetable, canola, coconut, whatever your preferred baking oil is)
- 1 1/2 teaspoons cinnamon
- 1 1/2 teaspoon vanilla extract
- chocolate covered coins OR colored chocolate candies
- paper lunch bags

Directions:
1. Preheat oven to 325 degrees F.
2. Line a large baking sheet with parchment paper.
3. Combine oats, oat bran, flax seed, seeds, pecans, and walnuts in a large bowl.
4. Combine brown sugar, honey, maple syrup, salt, oil, cinnamon, and vanilla in a medium saucepan and bring to a boil over medium heat.
5. Pour mixture over the dry ingredients. Thoroughly coat.
6. Spread out mixture onto parchment paper lined baking pan and bake at 325 degrees F for 15–20 minutes.
7. Toss the mixture once during the baking process.
8. Cool completely.
9. Separate the mixture into paper lunch bags and hide either the chocolate coins or the colored chocolate candies inside. This will represent that without his brothers' knowledge Joseph told his servants to place in their sacks the money his brothers had paid for the grain. They did not discover that this had been done until they stopped along the way home to spend the night.
10. Enjoy!

PART THREE
How God Protected His Chosen People
and Led Them Into the Promised Land

CHAPTER 6
God Calls Moses to Lead His People

LISTENING TO GOD'S WORD

Exodus 4:10-12

But Moses said to the Lord, "Oh, my Lord, I am not eloquent, either heretofore or since thou hast spoken to thy servant; but I am slow of speech and of tongue." Then the Lord said to him, "Who has made man's mouth? Who makes him dumb, or deaf, or seeing, or blind? Is it not I, the Lord? Now therefore go, and I will be with your mouth and teach you what you shall speak."

QUESTIONS FOR REVIEW

1. Name three terms used to identify God's chosen people.
   1. Israelites
   2. Hebrews
   3. Jews

2. Why did later pharaohs enslave Jacob's people?

   Later pharaohs were jealous of the strength and wealth of the Hebrews. They feared that the Hebrews might have ties with rivals of Egypt. They also needed slaves to build their temples, canals, and cities and the Hebrews made a huge work force.

3. How was Moses' mother protecting him when the pharaoh decreed that every Hebrew boy should be killed as soon as he was born? Did her plan work?

   She placed him in a basket and sent him down the Nile river and prayed that God would protect him. Yes, her plan worked. Pharaoh's daughter adopted Moses and raised him in the royal court with the protection of the palace.

4. **When was Moses given the mission to lead his people to freedom?**

   He was given the mission at the burning bush on Mount Horeb.

5. **Name the three miraculous signs that God gave to Moses to prove to the Hebrews that he was to be their leader.**
   1. Moses' staff turned into a serpent and then back into a staff again.
   2. Moses put his hand to his chest and it was covered with leprosy. Then he put it to his chest again and it was healed.
   3. Some water that Moses took from the Nile turned into blood.

6. **Name the first nine plagues that Egypt suffered.**
   1. water turned into blood
   2. frogs
   3. gnats
   4. flies
   5. livestock died
   6. boils
   7. hail
   8. locusts
   9. darkness

7. **Why did God send so many plagues?**

   He sent them because Pharaoh was stubborn and refused to yield to the first nine plagues.

NARRATION EXERCISES

Moses as a baby

Pharaoh decreed that every Hebrew baby boy should be killed as soon as it was born. Moses' mother protected him by placing him in a basket and sending him down the Nile river. She prayed for him. Pharaoh's daughter found Moses and raised him in the palace.

Moses' Mission

God spoke to Moses through a burning bush and gave him the mission to lead his people to freedom. Moses went to Pharaoh and told him to let his people go. Pharaoh refused and as a result God sent plagues.

CHAPTER 6: **God Calls Moses to Lead His People**

MAP ACTIVITY: MOSES BEGINS HIS MISSION

(Activity Book Page 61)

1. Draw a red line from Egypt to the region of Mt. Sinai. This shows Moses fleeing from Egypt after he had killed an Egyptian boss and was condemned to death himself.
2. Locate Mount Horeb and draw a burning bush. This is where Moses received his mission from God.
3. Draw a yellow line from Mount Horeb back to Egypt showing that God told Moses to go back to the land of Egypt and deliver his people from slavery.

Activity Projects

COLORING PAGES

Burning Bush *(Activity Book Page 57)*

Color the picture of the burning bush where God spoke to Moses.

CRAFT PROJECT 1: MOSES BASKET ON THE NILE

Materials:
- ☐ paper plate
- ☐ white muffin liner
- ☐ green construction paper
- ☐ modeling clay
- ☐ blue and brown markers
- ☐ stapler

Directions:

1. Color the paper plate blue (this will be our Nile River). You can add fish to the water if desired.
2. Color the muffin liner brown (this will be our basket for Moses) and glue in the center of the plate.
3. Cut an 8" x 3" section of green construction paper and staple along the edge of the plate (positioning does not matter).
4. Cut vertical slits in the green construction paper (these are our reeds along the banks of the Nile).
5. Mold a baby from the clay and allow to dry and harden. Use markers to create a face and blanket for baby Moses.
6. Place Moses in the middle of his basket.
7. Enjoy!

CRAFT PROJECT 2: BALANCE FROG FROM THE FROG PLAGUE

(Activity Book Page 59)

Materials
- ☐ Template from Activity Book
- ☐ green card stock paper (or white card stock colored green)
- ☐ scissors
- ☐ craft glue
- ☐ clear tape
- ☐ googly eyes
- ☐ 2 pennies

Directions:

1. Using the template in the Activity Book, cut your frog shape from the card stock paper.
2. Color your frog if using white card stock.
3. Glue the googly eyes onto the frog.
4. Tape a penny to the underside of each front leg of the frog.
5. Balance your frog on one finger by placing the mouth of the frog on your finger and allow the weight of the pennies to balance each other.
6. Enjoy!

SNACK PROJECT 1: FLIES PLAGUE DRINK

Ingredients/Materials:
- ☐ water
- ☐ ice cube tray
- ☐ mini plastic flies
- ☐ clear liquid drink such as apple juice, sprite, water, or lemonade
- ☐ clear drinking glass

Directions:

1. Place one plastic fly in each section of the ice cube tray.
2. Fill the ice cube tray with the flies with water.
3. Freeze over night.
4. Add the ice cubes with the "clear" liquid of choice to the clear glass.
5. Enjoy!

CHAPTER 7
The Escape from Egypt

LISTENING TO GOD'S WORD

Exodus 15:2

> The Lord is my strength and my song,
> and he has become my salvation;
> this is my God, and I will praise him,
> my father's God, and I will exalt him.

QUESTIONS FOR REVIEW

1. **What was the tenth plague? How were the Hebrews spared this plague?**

   All the firstborn Egyptian children were to die. The Hebrews spread the blood of the Passover lamb on the doorposts and the destroying angel passed over their homes. Not a single Hebrew child was slain.

2. **To lead the way for them, what did the Lord appear to the Hebrew people as by day? And by night?**

   He appeared as a pillar of cloud by day and a pillar of fire by night.

3. **What happened at the Red Sea that allowed the Hebrews to escape the Egyptian army?**

   God commanded Moses to lift up his rod so that the sea would part and the Hebrews could cross on dry land. When they had crossed, God commanded Moses to again stretch out his hand so that the waters would close in on the Egyptians.

4. **When God heard the Hebrews complaining about Moses and about their hunger, how did He respond?**

   He sent manna and quail to them through a miracle.

5. **When God heard the Hebrews complaining that they were thirsty, how did He respond?**

   He commanded Moses to strike a rock and when Moses did this, water came rushing forth.

6. **What did Moses have to do in order to win the battle with the Amalekites?**

   He had to hold his staff above his head as he prayed, as long as he did this the Israelites were successful, but if it lowered, the Israelites gave way to the enemy.

NARRATION EXERCISES

The First Passover

The final plague on the Egyptians was that the first born of every household would die. God commanded the Israelites to kill a lamb and put its blood over their doorways. In this way, the destroying angel would know not to enter their homes. Not a single Hebrew child was slain.

The Flight from Egypt

Pharaoh finally agreed to let the Israelites go. They left Egypt, but Pharaoh changed his mind and sent his army after them. When the Israelites reached the Red Sea, Moses held up his staff and stretched out his hand and the waters parted allowing them passage through. Once they were on the other side, Moses again stretched out his hand and the waters came crashing down on the Egyptians.

MAP ACTIVITY: THE ISRAELITES' EXODUS FROM EGYPT

(Activity Book Page 67)

1. Trace the portion of the already drawn route from the Land of Goshen to Mount Horeb.
2. Where the route crosses the Red Sea, draw Moses' staff to show that this is where God worked the miracle of the parting of the sea.

CHAPTER 7: **The Escape from Egypt**

Activity Projects

COLORING PAGE

Parting the Red Sea *(Activity Book Page 63)*
Color the picture of the parting of the Red Sea and the Israelites escaping the Egyptian army.

WORD SEARCH

Escape from Egypt *(Activity Book Pages 65–66)*
Fill in the blanks for the Escape from Egypt word search clues and then find the corresponding words in the word search. *Note:* There is a word bank at the end of the word search to aid the student.

Word Search Answer Key:

1. gold
2. firstborn
3. Passover
4. doorposts
5. destroyer
6. pursued
7. rod
8. walls
9. stretched
10. desert
11. bread
12. rock
13. staff
14. Jethro
15. Judges

CRAFT PROJECT 1: PILLAR OF CLOUD AND PILLAR OF FIRE

To show them the way, the Lord appeared to them by day as a pillar of cloud, and by night as a pillar of fire.

Materials:
- ☐ 2 paper towel rolls
- ☐ craft glue
- ☐ cotton balls
- ☐ red, yellow, and orange tissue OR construction paper
- ☐ scissors

Directions:
1. Glue one side of each cotton ball and adhere it to the first paper towel roll. This is the pillar of cloud.

65

2. Cut the tissue or construction paper into small squares and slightly crumble.
3. Place glue on one side of each piece and adhere them to the second of paper towel roll. This is the pillar of fire.
4. Enjoy!

SNACK PROJECT 1: PARTING THE RED SEA CARROT MUFFIN

Ingredients:
- ☐ 1 1/3 cup all purpose flour
- ☐ 1 1/2 teaspoons baking soda
- ☐ 1 1/4 teaspoons baking powder
- ☐ 1 1/2 teaspoons cinnamon
- ☐ 1/2 teaspoon salt
- ☐ 3 eggs
- ☐ 1 cup white sugar
- ☐ 3/4 cup vegetable, canola, coconut, or other preferred baking oil
- ☐ 1 teaspoon vanilla
- ☐ 1 1/2 cups grated carrot
- ☐ 1/2 cup shredded apple
- ☐ 1/4 cup cream cheese
- ☐ 2 tablespoons softened butter
- ☐ 1 teaspoon vanilla extract
- ☐ 1 1/2 cups sifted confectioners sugar
- ☐ blue food coloring
- ☐ gummy bears

Directions:
1. Preheat oven to 325 degrees F.
2. Grease the bottoms of 12 muffin cups or line with 12 baking cups.
3. Sift flour, baking soda, baking powder, cinnamon, and salt together in a large bowl.
4. In a separate bowl, beat eggs and sugar until fluffy. Stir in the oil, vanilla, carrot, and apple.
5. Fold the flour mixture into the wet mixture.
6. Evenly separate the batter into the muffin cups.
7. Bake for 15–20 minutes. A toothpick inserted in the middle should come out clean.
8. Allow to cool completely.
9. Beat together the cream cheese, butter, vanilla, and confectioner's sugar until fluffy.
10. Tint with the blue food coloring until desired shade of blue.
11. Frost both sides of the cooled muffin leaving a centerline where the muffin itself is visible (this will be the track the Israelites took).

12. Use your gummy bears to march through the red sea.
13. Place several gummy bears in the middle of the muffin and then ice on top of these gummy bears (this is the sea covering the Egyptians).
14. Enjoy your snack!

SNACK PROJECT 2: MANNA PIE CRUST

Ingredients:
- ☐ pre-made pie crust
- ☐ 1/2 cup room temperature butter
- ☐ 1/3 cup honey

Directions:
1. Pre-heat oven to 350 degrees F.
2. Cut the pre-made pie crust into small circular shapes.
3. Line a baking sheet with parchment paper.
4. Place small circular pie crust cut outs on the baking sheet.
5. Bake for approximately 10 minutes. Watch carefully as the baking time will depend somewhat on the size of your circle.
6. Beat together the butter and honey.
7. Brush the honey butter onto your circular pie crust cut-outs.
8. Enjoy!

CHAPTER 8
The Revelation of God's Law

LISTENING TO GOD'S WORD

Exodus 20:1-3

And God spoke all these words, saying,

"I am the Lord your God, who brought you out of the land of Egypt, out of the house of bondage.

"You shall have no other gods before me."

QUESTIONS FOR REVIEW

1. Name the 10 commandments:

"I am the Lord your God, who brought you out of the land of Egypt. . . . You shall have no other gods before Me."
"You shall not take the name of the Lord your God in vain."
"Remember the Sabbath day, to keep it holy."
"Honor your father and your mother."
"You shall not kill."
"You shall not commit adultery."
"You shall not steal."
"You shall not bear false witness against your neighbor."
"You shall not covet your neighbor's wife."
"You shall not covet your neighbor's house . . . or anything that is your neighbor's."

2. What did the people hear and see at Mount Sinai when God gave Moses the Law?

- lightening
- thunder
- heavy cloud
- trumpet blast
- earthquake
- thick smoke

3. **What did the people do when Moses stayed on the mountain for forty days and forty nights?**

   They feared that God had abandoned them so they began to worship an idol instead.

4. **What happened when Moses came down the mountain and saw the Israelites worshiping an idol?**

   He was furious and shattered the two tablets on which the Ten Commandments had been written. He burnt the idol and beat it into powder, and then he commanded that those who had led the idol worship should be killed. He asked God's people to stand with him and immediately the sons of Levi did. They drew their swords and slew the guilty.

5. **What is the correlation between ancient worship rituals and many of our Christian worship practices today?**

   Jesus Christ is the fulfillment of God's promise to his chosen people. Many of those rituals find their fulfillment in Jesus.

NARRATION EXERCISES

The Ten Commandments

God gave Moses the Ten Commandments on Mount Sinai. A heavy cloud covered the mountain. The earth quaked and a trumpet sounded. Then God's voice was heard proclaiming the Commandments. Moses went up the mountain and God gave him the Commandments written on stone. While he was gone some of the people began to worship an idol. Moses was furious and he threw and broke the tablets on which the Commandments were written. Moses sentenced the leaders of the idol worship to death. Moses went back up the mountain and again God wrote the Ten Commandments on two tablets.

CHAPTER 8: **The Revelation of God's Law**

MAP ACTIVITY: THE TEN COMMANDMENTS

(Activity Page 79)

1. At Mount Sinai, draw two tablets that are to represent the Ten Commandments.

Activity Projects

COLORING PAGES

Moses and the Ten Commandments *(Activity Page 69)*
   Color the picture of Moses holding the Ten Commandments, which were given to him by God.

Lamb of Sacrifice *(Activity Page 71)*
   Color the picture of the lamb the Israelites ate on the evening of Passover.

CRAFT PROJECT 1: THE TEN COMMANDMENTS

(Activity Book Pages 73–75)

Materials:
- ☐ Templates from Activity Book
- ☐ 4 sheets of gray or brown construction paper
- ☐ scissors
- ☐ craft glue
- ☐ clear tape

Directions

1. Using 4 full sheets of construction paper, copy the tablet template and cut it out. Each tablet gets 5 commandments. You will end up with 2 full sets of commandments.
2. Cut out the commandments and paste them to the tablets.
3. Cut one set of commandments into several pieces and then tape together (this is the first set of commandments that Moses broke).
4. The second set is from Moses' second trip up the mount.
5. Enjoy!

CRAFT PROJECT 2: TEN COMMANDMENTS DISCOVERY BAG

Materials:
1. A first place ribbon, trophy, medal, or a number 1 cut out by teacher. This symbolizes that God is to be first in our life.
2. Small tube of toothpaste or small container of mouthwash. This symbolizes that we are to keep our mouth clean by not using God's name in vain.
3. Photo of Mom and Dad. This symbolizes that you are to honor your father and mother.
4. A paper calendar with Sundays and Holy Days of Obligation circled in red. This symbolizes the commandment requiring you to keep holy the Sabbath and other Holy Days.
5. Plastic knife, pretend knife, or other weapon. This symbolizes that you should not kill.
6. A heart shape broken into 2 pieces (feel free to omit as this commandment may or may not be one you have covered with your children). This symbolizes the commandment forbidding adultery.
7. Cut a hand shape out of the construction paper and tape a piece of candy to the palm. This symbolizes that you are not to steal.
8. A strip of paper that says "lie, lie, lie" with each word increasing in size and in darkness (in other words, the lie grows as the further down the strip it gets). This symbolizes that you should not to bear false witness against your neighbor.
9. Two rings, plastic or real. This symbolizes the sacredness of marriage and the commitment. This will cover the ninth commandment. Here the emphasis will be on husband and wife appreciating and focusing on one another as they did the day they were married.
10. A piece of jewelry or other pretty object that the child might see as something special. This symbolizes that you should not to covet your neighbor's goods.
11. Pillowcase

Directions:
1. Place all items in the pillowcase and allow the child to draw out one item at a time and name the commandment that the object symbolizes. If the child guesses "wrong" they may have a reason for doing so. Talk it through and ask if another commandment might fit as well.

CHAPTER 8: **The Revelation of God's Law**

SNACK PROJECT 1: TEN COMMANDMENT COOKIES

Ingredients:
- ☐ 12 tablespoons softened butter
- ☐ 2 1/2 cups powdered sugar
- ☐ 6 egg whites
- ☐ 2 tablespoons vanilla extract
- ☐ 2 teaspoons almond extract
- ☐ 1 1/2 cup flour
- ☐ 16 oz. bittersweet chocolate, chopped
- ☐ 1 cup heavy cream
- ☐ 1/2 cup unsalted butter
- ☐ freezer bag with corner cut off OR piping bag with 1/4" plain tip

Directions:
1. Preheat oven to 350 degrees F.
2. Cream butter.
3. Incorporate powdered sugar and mix thoroughly.
4. Slowly beat in egg whites.
5. Add vanilla and mix.
6. Slowly add in flour, mixing just well enough to combine.
7. Fill piping bag or freezer bag with mix and pipe out 3 in. sections onto a baking sheet (keep in mind that these are going to be tablet shaped).
8. Bake for about 10 minutes or until a light golden brown.
9. In a small saucepan, heat cream and butter over medium-high stirring continuously until boiling.
10. Once this mixture begins to boil, pour it onto the chocolate chunks.
11. Wait a few seconds and once chocolate is melting, stir continuously until it is completely melted.
12. Allow mixture to cool and set up.
13. Completely coat one side of the cooled cookie with the cooled chocolate filling and then press another cookie to it, forming a sandwich.
14. Using a small tip piping bag or a freezer bag with a small corner cut, pipe on the roman numerals I, II, III, IV, and V.
15. Repeat the process with next two cookies and filling adding the roman numerals VI, VII, VIII, IX, and X.
16. Make as many sets of ten commandments as you like.
17. Enjoy!

CROSSWORD PUZZLE

The Ten Commandments *(Activity Page 77)*

Across:
2. two
6. importance
7. covet
8. witness
11. Sabbath
12. vain

Down:
1. boundary
3. before
4. obedient
5. voice
9. Sinai
10. Canaan

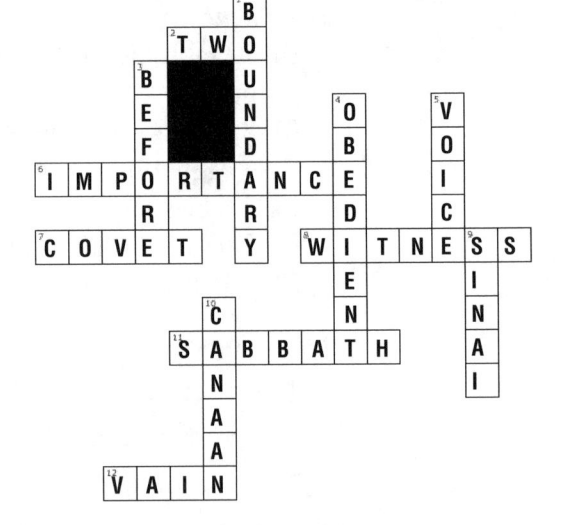

CHAPTER 9
The Desert Wanderings of the Israelites

LISTENING TO GOD'S WORD

Exodus 33:14

And he said, "My presence will go with you, and I will give you rest."

QUESTIONS FOR REVIEW

1. When God's presence lifted into the heavens as a sign that it was once again time to travel on, how did the group of Israelites proceed?

   The Ark of the Covenant was carried first followed by the materials for the Tabernacle.

2. Why did God command Moses to choose twelve men, one from each tribe?

   They were to be sent as scouts, or spies, into the land of Canaan.

3. Why did the Israelites refuse to enter the Promised Land? What was their punishment for this refusal?

   They refused to enter the Promised Land because they feared the people who lived there. All who were over 20 years of age were condemned to linger in the desert until they died.

4. Name 3 of the punishments that God sent in response to the people complaining.
   1. fire
   2. plague
   3. venomous snakes

5. Why was Moses prevented from entering the Promised Land?

   Moses had disobeyed God by the way that he gave the people water at Kadesh.

6. How did Balaam's donkey save his life?

    The donkey refused to go forward when he saw a threatening angel blocking the path ahead.

NARRATION EXERCISES

Wandering in the Desert

The Israelites left Mount Sinai and headed to the land of Canaan. When they got there, the people refused to enter because they were afraid of the people who lived there. For their punishment, all who were over the age of twenty were condemned to linger in the desert until they died.

Balaam

God spoke to Balaam and at first told him not to go with King Balak to curse the people of Israel. When King Balak asked Balaam again, God told Balaam to go. On the road, an angel stood with his sword drawn. Balaam could not see the angel but Balaam's donkey could and the donkey refused to pass. Balaam beat his donkey three times before he saw the angel and understood. The angel instructed Balaam to go with the king but not to curse the Israelites. Balaam blessed the Israelites instead of cursing them.

MAP ACTIVITY: THE DESERT WANDERINGS

(Activity Book Page 83)

1. Trace the already drawn route of the Israelites beginning at Mount Sinai and going to the edge of the map.
2. This is a good time to note what a long and tedious journey it must have been.

Activity Projects

COLORING PAGE

Balaam and his donkey *(Activity Book Page 81)*

Color the picture of Balaam and the donkey that saved his life.

CHAPTER 9: **The Desert Wanderings of the Israelites**

CRAFT PROJECT 1: VENOMOUS SNAKE (ONE OF THE PUNISHMENTS)

Materials:
- ☐ construction paper in the colors you want for your snake
- ☐ stapler OR clear tape
- ☐ googly eyes
- ☐ craft glue
- ☐ small piece of red construction paper (for tongue)

Directions:

1. Cut 8" x 2" strips from the construction paper.
2. Staple or tape the first strip into a loop.
3. Connect the second loop to the first and continue on until snake is of desired length (this will form a paper chain).
4. Cut a small rectangle from red construction paper and cut a slit at one end. Attach to the head of your snake (this will be the snake's tongue).
5. Glue googly eyes above the tongue.
6. Enjoy!

CRAFT PROJECT 2: BALAAM AND HIS DONKEY

(Activity Book Page 81)

Materials:
- ☐ Template from Activity Book
- ☐ 2 popsicle sticks
- ☐ craft glue OR clear tape
- ☐ colored pencils

Directions:

1. Color Balaam on his donkey and the angel from the template.
2. Cut out the colored figures.
3. Glue or tape your figures to the popsicle sticks.
4. Act out the story of Balaam and the angel.
5. Enjoy!

SNACK PROJECT 1: 12 "GINGERBREAD" MEN SENT AS SPIES

Ingredients:
- 1 (3.5 oz.) package of cook-and-serve butterscotch pudding mix
- 1/2 cup of butter
- 1/2 cup packed light brown sugar
- 1 egg
- 1 1/2 cups all purpose flour
- 1/2 teaspoon baking soda
- 1 1/2 teaspoons ground ginger
- 3/4 teaspoon ground cinnamon
- 4 cups confectioners sugar
- 1/2 cup shortening
- 5 tablespoons milk
- 1 teaspoon vanilla extract
- green food coloring

Directions:
1. Cream together the pudding mix, butter, and brown sugar until smooth.
2. Beat in the egg.
3. In a separate bowl, sift together the flour, baking soda, ginger, and cinnamon.
4. Mix the dry ingredients with the wet ingredients.
5. Cover and chill until dough firms (around an hour).
6. Preheat the oven to 325 degrees F.
7. Line a baking sheet with parchment paper.
8. Flour your cutting surface and roll out dough to 1/8" thickness.
9. Using a gingerbread man cookie cutter, cut out your shapes.
10. Place the men on the baking sheet lined with parchment paper.
11. Bake for approximately 10 minutes or until a light golden brown.
12. Cool completely.
13. In a large bowl, cream together the confectioner's sugar and shortening until smooth.
14. Gradually mix in the milk and vanilla until smooth and stiff.
15. Add green food coloring to the icing.
16. Decorate your "spies" in green icing so that they are camouflaged.
17. Enjoy!

CHAPTER 10
Joshua, Commander of the Israelites

LISTENING TO GOD'S WORD

Joshua 1:9

"Have I not commanded you? Be strong and of good courage; be not frightened, neither be dismayed; for the Lord your God is with you wherever you go."

QUESTIONS FOR REVIEW

1. **What lay North, South, East, and West of Canaan?**
   North—the mountainous lands of what is now Lebanon
   South—the Sinai Desert, a part of Egypt
   East—the Dead Sea and the Great Eastern Desert
   West—the coastal area of the Mediterranean Sea

2. **What were the two seasons in Canaan?**
   The two seasons were the rainy season and the dry season.

3. **Of all the people who lived in Canaan when Joshua led the Israelites across the Jordan, who was the most powerful? What were their weapons made of that gave them an advantage?**
   The Philistines who had weapons made of iron instead of bronze.

4. **How did the Israelites cross the Jordan River into Canaan?**
   The priests carried the Ark of the Covenant into the river, and a dry path appeared for the people to cross.

5. What did the Lord instruct Joshua to have his army do in order to conquer the city of Jericho?

   The Lord instructed Joshua to send forty thousand fighting men to march around the walls of the city every day for six days. On the seventh day, the soldiers, the priests carrying the Ark of the Covenant, and all the Israelites marched around the walls seven times. At the end of the seventh time around the city, Joshua gave the command, "Shout, for the Lord has given you the city." At that moment seven trumpets sounded a continuous blast, the people gave a mighty shout, and the walls fell!

6. How did Joshua gain victory over the Amorites at Gibeon?

   At his command, the sun and moon both stood still, giving him the extra time he needed.

NARRATION EXERCISES

Jericho

The Lord told Joshua to have forty thousand men march around the city of Jericho each day for six days. On the seventh day, the soldiers, the priests carrying the Ark of the Covenant, and all the Israelites marched around the walls seven times. At the end of the seventh time around the city, Joshua gave the command to give a shout. At that moment trumpets sounded a continual blast and the people all gave a mighty shout and the walls of Jericho fell.

MAP ACTIVITY: CANAAN'S EARLY INHABITANTS

(Activity Page 87)

1. On the map of Canaan's early inhabitants, locate the area that the Philistines lived in. Color this area red. The Philistines were the most powerful of the peoples in Canaan at the time that the Israelites came to Canaan.
2. Next locate the area where the Phoenicians dwelled. The Phoenicians lived along the coast and are believed to be the first to develop an alphabet. Color their land green.
3. Now locate the Moabites. The Moabites are named after Moab, the son of Lot. Color this area orange.

CHAPTER 10: **Joshua, Commander of the Israelites**

4. Next find the land of the Amorites who were descendants of Cain. Color their area in yellow.
5. Now find the land of the Edomites. These people were descendants of Esau. They lived south of the Dead Sea. The Amorites drove them south. Color their region light blue.
6. Locate the city of Jericho. Draw a wall around the city to show the fortifications that were there when Joshua arrived. Draw also a trumpet near the city to show that it was conquered by obeying the Lord and marching around the city. On the final lap the trumpets were blown and a loud cry was let out and the walls of this great fortification fell!

Activity Projects

COLORING PAGE

Joshua *(Activity Book Page 85)*
Color the picture of Joshua, the commander of the Israelites.

CRAFT PROJECT 1: TRUMPET AT JERICHO

Materials:
- ☐ paper towel roll
- ☐ markers
- ☐ scissors
- ☐ 4 buttons
- ☐ hot glue gun

Directions:
1. Color the paper towel roll any colors you would like your trumpet to be.
2. Cut 5, 3 in. slits along one end of the paper towel roll.
3. Glue the 4 buttons into place to be the trumpet keys.
4. Enjoy!

CRAFT PROJECT 2: BUILD THE WALL OF JERICHO

Materials:
- ☐ Lincoln logs OR wooden blocks OR Legos OR any other building block you have
- ☐ soldier figures OR Lego men OR stuffed animals OR any other figures you have to use as the army

Directions:
1. Build a fort out of whatever type of building blocks you have.
2. March your figures around the wall 1 time each day for 6 days and then 7 times on the 7th day.
3. Give a shout and use your trumpet from the craft project in this chapter.
4. It's time to wreck the wall! Knock the wall down and conquer the city.
5. Enjoy!

SNACK PROJECT 1: GRAHAM CRACKER JERICHO

Ingredients:
- ☐ sandwich bread
- ☐ graham crackers
- ☐ peanut butter or almond butter
- ☐ gummy bears

Directions:
1. Make a peanut butter or almond butter sandwich. Coat the outside crust with more peanut or almond butter.
2. Break your graham crackers along lines.
3. Line up each graham cracker piece vertically along the outside of the sandwich (this is our wall around Jericho so the graham cracker should be taller than the sandwich. The peanut or almond butter is our bonding agent to keep the graham crackers from falling).
4. March the gummy bears around the outside wall.
5. On the final lap every one gives a shout and you knock down the graham cracker wall.
6. Enjoy your snack!

CHAPTER 11
The Israelites in the Promised Land

LISTENING TO GOD'S WORD

1 Samuel 3:10

And the Lord came and stood forth, calling as at other times, "Samuel! Samuel!" And Samuel said, "Speak, for thy servant hears."

QUESTIONS FOR REVIEW

1. Name some of the principal adversaries of the Israelites.
   - Philistines
   - Moabites
   - Hittites
   - Midianites
   - Ammonites
   - Canaanites

2. Why did God permit the enemies of the Israelites to wage war against them?

   He was chastising the Israelites for failing to keep His commandments after they settled into their new life in Canaan.

3. Of the thirty-two thousand men Gideon had raised to protect the Israelites, how many did God tell him to keep and why?

   God had him choose only three hundred of the men because these were the men who drank from the river from the cupped palms of their hands showing that even while they were drinking they were keeping an eye out for the enemy.

4. **What did the Israelites use to confuse and defeat the Midianites in the Valley of Esdraelon?**

   They used trumpets, pitchers, and lamps that made the Midianites, in the darkness, think that they were surrounded. They fled in a panic killing one another along the way. Gideon and his army pursued them and won victory.

5. **Why did Gideon refuse to be king?**

   They had the Lord as their king and did not need an earthly king.

6. **Name some of the weapons Samson used against the Philistines.**
   - burning foxes
   - the jawbone of a donkey
   - the roof and pillars of a banquet hall

7. **What was the source of Samson's strength?**

   The source of his strength was his hair that had never been cut as a vow of consecration to God.

8. **How is it that Samuel came to live with Eli at the Tabernacle?**

   Samuel's mother Hannah had wept furiously before the Tabernacle and promised that if she was to have a son she would consecrate him to God all the days of his life. Upon his birth, Hannah remembered her promise and took him to Eli.

9. **What important role did Ruth play in salvation history?**

   Her son would one day become the grandfather of David the king, and through his family would come the Savior.

NARRATION EXERCISES

Gideon

Gideon was an honorable man of God. God promised Gideon victory over the invaders. Gideon asked God for a sign. Gideon placed a fleece on the ground and the next morning there was dew on the fleece but none on the ground. The following day there was dew on the ground but none on the fleece. In this way Gideon was reassured of God's promise of protection.

Samson

Samson was dedicated by his parents to the service of God. He was separated and was not to drink strong drink or to cut his hair. Samson

CHAPTER 11: **The Israelites in the Promised Land**

had incredible strength and fought the Philistines. Samson revealed the source of his strength to Delilah who cut his hair. He was then captured by the Philistines, blinded, and thrown into prison. His hair grew back and when he was brought out of prison to be made fun of, Samson destroyed the banquet hall by shaking the pillars.

Samuel Speaks to God

Samuel lived with the high priest, Eli, at the Tabernacle. One night God spoke to Samuel and told Samuel that Eli's sons would be punished for their wickedness and that Eli would be punished because he neglected to discipline his children.

MAP ACTIVITY: GIDEON, SAMSON, AND SAMUEL

(Activity Book Page 97)

1. Locate the Plain of Esdraelon. This is where Gideon led an army of three hundred to conquer the great Midianite army. Draw a trumpet, a pitcher, and a torch to show how Gideon's army deceived the Midianites into believing that they were surrounded by a vast army.
2. Locate the land of the Philistines. Draw a fox in this land to remind you of the story of Samson tying the foxes together and attaching torches to them, thus burning the corn fields, the grape vineyards, and the olives on the trees.
3. Circle the city of Gaza to show both where Samson slept and literally broke out of the city by taking the gates with their posts with him and where Samson later became imprisoned after being tricked by Delilah.
4. Locate the city of Shiloh and circle it with yellow. This is where Samuel was raised and where the Ark of the Covenant was kept until the Philistines captured it.

Activity Projects

COLORING PAGE

Samson *(Activity Book Page 89)*

Color the picture of Samson as he destroys the banquet hall by shaking the pillars.

Story of the Bible: The Old Testament **TEACHER'S MANUAL**

MAZE: HELP SAMSON ESCAPE GAZA

(Activity Book Page 91)

Help Samson Escape Gaza Maze Answer Key

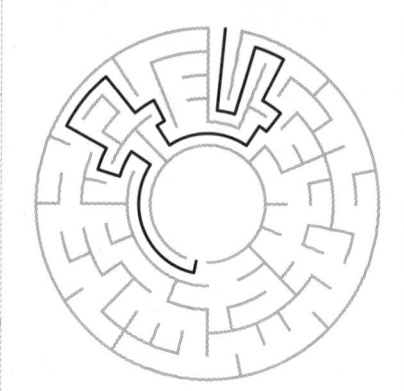

RUTH WORD SEARCH

(Activity Book Page 95–96)

Fill in the blanks for the Ruth word search clues and then find the corresponding words in the word search. Note: There is a word bank at the end of the word search to aid the student.

Word Search Answer Key

1. leave
2. lodge
3. people
4. God
5. Bethlehem
6. Boaz
7. kindness
8. love
9. house
10. Obed
11. grandfather
12. Savior

CRAFT PROJECT 1: A TORCH FOR GIDEON

Materials:
- ☐ paper towel tube
- ☐ paper or styrofoam cup
- ☐ aluminum foil
- ☐ craft knife OR scissors
- ☐ red, yellow, and orange tissue OR construction paper
- ☐ craft glue

Directions:

1. Place the paper towel roll on the bottom of the cup and trace around the outside of the paper towel roll.
2. Cut out the circle from the bottom of the cup.
3. Insert the paper towel roll into the hole. Push the paper towel roll until it is almost flush with the top of the cup.
4. Wrap the paper towel roll and cup completely with aluminum foil.
5. Cut strips from the tissue OR construction paper and glue them to the inside of the cup.
6. Enjoy!

CHAPTER 11: **The Israelites in the Promised Land**

CRAFT PROJECT 2: HAIR GROWING SAMSON SPOON

(Activity Book Page 93)

Materials:
- ☐ 1, 10 in. wooden craft spoon
- ☐ craft glue
- ☐ brown yarn
- ☐ hole punch
- ☐ scissors
- ☐ 2 hole punch reinforcements (colored brown)
- ☐ markers
- ☐ hot glue gun
- ☐ Template from Activity Book

Directions:
1. Cut out and color Samson's body from the Activity Book. Hot glue the body onto the spoon.
2. Cut out the semi-circle template from the Activity Book and color it brown. Hole punch the semi-circle towards the top and add your reinforcements to both the front and back.
3. Hot glue this to the top of Samson's head. Make sure your hole is not covered by the spoon.
4. Cut 6 pieces of yarn to 10 in. in length.
5. Thread the yarn through the hole and tie a knot at the ends of each piece (to keep them from falling backwards through the hole), and tie them together on the backside of the spoon.
6. Draw a face for Samson.
7. Pull the hair back and forth through the hole to show how his hair was cut and then grew back while he was in prison.
8. Enjoy!

SCIENCE PROJECT 1: SAMSON'S GRASS HEAD

Materials:
- ☐ small plastic cup
- ☐ old pair of nylon stockings or knee-highs
- ☐ grass or alfalfa seeds
- ☐ potting soil
- ☐ googly eyes
- ☐ black felt square (or other black material)
- ☐ red felt square (or other red material)
- ☐ brown felt square (or other brown material)
- ☐ hot glue gun

Directions:
1. Cut a 10 in. section of the nylon stockings (make sure the toe is included).
2. Stretch the stocking over the opening to a glass or mug and spoon a teaspoon of the grass or alfalfa seeds into the stocking.

3. Fill the remainder with potting soil (to about a softball size).
4. Tie a knot to close the stocking.
5. This will be Samson's head. The excess fabric will go at the bottom and the top of his head will be where are seeds are located.
6. Make the nose and ears by pulling away small sections of the stocking/soil and twisting them into balls, two for the ears and one for the nose.
7. Cover the outside of the plastic cup with the brown material and hot glue into place.
8. Place the head, excess stocking side down, into the plastic cup container.
9. Use the hot glue gun to adhere googly eyes above Samson's nose.
10. Fashion eyebrows from the remaining brown fabric and hot glue into place.
11. Fashion lips from the red fabric and hot glue into place.
12. Dunk the head in a bowl of water and half fill the plastic cup with water. Make sure the excess stocking is sitting in the standing water in the plastic cup.
13. Place the Samson head in a window or somewhere where it will get plenty of light.
14. Check daily to make sure it stays moist.
15. It should begin to sprout in about a week. You will have enough hair for a haircut within 4 weeks.
16. Enjoy!

The science lesson here is on what plants need to grow. The student should be able to pinpoint water, sunlight, nutrients, and air as essential for the growth of the Samson head.

PART FOUR
How God's Chosen People Lived Under Their Kings

CHAPTER 12
Saul and David

LISTENING TO GOD'S WORD

1 Samuel 15:22

And Samuel said,

"Has the Lord as great delight in burnt offerings and sacrifices,
    as in obeying the voice of the Lord?
Behold, to obey is better than sacrifice,
    and to hearken than the fat of rams."

QUESTIONS FOR REVIEW

1. **Name some reasons that the Israelites wanted to be ruled by a king.**
   - They wanted to be united under one leader like the other nations around them.
   - They wanted a human king to lead them to a final victory of the Canaanites and the Philistines.
   - They thought a human king could prevent civil war.
   - They thought a human king could ensure justice.

2. **What lesson did Samuel give to Saul when he disobeyed? What were the consequences of Saul's actions?**

   The lesson is that "to obey is better than to sacrifice" and the consequence was "because you have rejected the word of the Lord, He has also rejected you from being king."

3. **Who was anointed to be become king after Saul?**

   David

4. How did David defeat Goliath?

    David defeated Goliath by using a slingshot and stone. The stone struck Goliath between the eyes and David ran up to him and cut off his head with his sword.

5. What was Saul's reaction to David's accomplishments? What did Saul do?

    Saul was very jealous of David and attempted to kill him on several occasions.

6. How did David demonstrate that he did not bear malice against Saul despite Saul's desire to kill David?

    David twice spared the life of Saul.

7. What did the ghost of Samuel prophesy would happen to Saul? What was David's reaction when the prophesy was fulfilled?

    Samuel said that Saul and his sons would die in battle. David mourned and wept and fasted until evening when Saul and his sons were indeed killed.

NARRATION EXERCISES

David and Goliath

David was bringing food to his brothers when he heard the shout and challenge of Goliath. David went to King Saul and said that he would fight Goliath. David was only a boy and Goliath was a giant, but David had confidence because he knew that God was on his side. David was allowed to fight. He hit Goliath in between the eyes using a slingshot and a stone. When Goliath fell, David cut off his head.

King Saul

Saul was chosen as king, but he disobeyed God and was told that the kingship would pass from his household. Saul loved David but was very jealous of him and on several occasions attempted to kill him.

MAP ACTIVITY: DAVID'S BEGINNINGS *(Activity Book Page 107)*

1. Locate Bethlehem on the map and draw a shepherd's crook and a crown here to show that David the shepherd boy was anointed by Samuel to become king.

CHAPTER 12: **Saul and David**

2. Find the Valley of Elah and draw a slingshot and 5 smooth stones to show this is the place where David defeated the great giant Goliath.

Activity Projects

COLORING PAGE

David and Goliath *(Activity Book Page 99)*
Color the picture of David fighting the giant Goliath with nothing more than a slingshot.

CRAFT PROJECT 1: DAVID'S MARSHMALLOW SLINGSHOT

Materials:
- 2 empty toilet paper rolls
- 2 large rubber bands (do not need to be thick)
- pencil
- strong tape (such as duct tape)
- hole punch reinforcements
- mini marshmallows

Directions:
1. Cut the toilet paper roll in half lengthwise.
2. Roll half the toilet paper roll into a tight cylinder.
3. Completely wrap the cylinder with strong tape.
4. Make a small hole completely through the diameter of the cylinder and insert the pencil into this hole.
5. Cut the rubber band in half and attach to one end of the pencil.
6. Repeat with second rubber band and other side of the pencil.
7. Cut a 3"x 5" rectangular section from the remaining toilet paper roll and fold in half so that it now measures 1 1/2"x 2 1/2".
8. Place a small piece of duct tape to hold together the open side.
9. Hole punch each end and place hole punch reinforcements around the holes.
10. Attach the free ends of the rubber bands to the "pouch" and knot in place.
11. Load with marshmallows.
12. Enjoy!

Story of the Bible: The Old Testament **TEACHER'S MANUAL**

CRAFT PROJECT 2: TOILET PAPER ROLL DAVID AND PAPER TOWEL ROLL GOLIATH

(Activity Book Page 101–103)

Materials:
☐ Templates from Activity Book
☐ coloring pencils
☐ craft glue
☐ scissors
☐ empty paper towel roll
☐ empty toilet paper roll

Directions:

1. Remove the templates from the Activity Book and color the David and Goliath figures.
2. For David, cut along the dotted lines to fit size of toilet paper roll.
3. For Goliath, just use the page as is. Minimal trimming or none at all should be needed.
3. Use craft glue to attach David and Goliath to the rolls.
4. Enjoy!

DAVID WORD SEARCH

(Activity Book Page 105)

Word Search Answer Key

1. anointed
2. armor
3. Bethlehem
4. David
5. God
6. Goliath
7. harp
8. helmet
9. Jonathan
10. King
11. Lord
12. music
13. Philistine
14. Samuel
15. servant
16. Saul
16. sling
17. spear
18. stones
19. sword

CHAPTER 13
David's Reign

LISTENING TO GOD'S WORD

Psalm 23

> The Lord is my shepherd, I shall not want;
>   he makes me lie down in green pastures.
> He leads me beside still waters;
>   he restores my soul.
> He leads me in paths of righteousness
>   for his name's sake.
>
> Even though I walk through the valley of the shadow of death,
>   I fear no evil;
> for thou art with me;
>   thy rod and thy staff,
>   they comfort me.
>
> Thou preparest a table before me
>   in the presence of my enemies;
> thou anointest my head with oil,
>   my cup overflows.
> Surely goodness and mercy shall follow me
>   all the days of my life;
> and I shall dwell in the house of the Lord
>   for ever.

QUESTIONS FOR REVIEW

1. What city did David decide to make the capital? How did he establish this city?
   The city was Jerusalem and he captured it from the Canaanites.

2. **What did David bring to the capital city in order to attach the people more closely to himself and to the capital?**

   The Ark of the Covenant

3. **What happened to David's son, Absalom, when he revolted and attempted to seize the throne for himself?**

   While riding away on a mule, Absalom's long hair was caught in the branch of a tree. He was jerked from the mule's back and left hanging in the air. Joab, the captain of David's army, found him there and thrust three lances into his heart.

4. **What action did David take against Uriah in order to take his wife Bathsheba?**

   He gave orders for Uriah to be placed in the front line of battle. Then he commanded Uriah's fellow soldiers to fall back and leave him there alone to be killed.

5. **What did the prophet Nathan point out to David in the story of the rich and the poor man and the little lamb? How did David respond?**

   Nathan pointed out David's sinfulness. David was immediately sorry for his sin and asked for God's forgiveness.

6. **Name some of David's accomplishments.**
   - He united the Israelites into one great nation.
   - He created a large standing army with experienced commanders.
   - He organized the Levites to care for the Ark, guarded the treasures collected for the Temple, and formed a choir to chant sacred music.
   - He collected supplies for the building of a magnificent Temple for the worship of God, though he was not to be the one who built it.

NARRATION EXERCISES

David as King

David was a very good king. He obeyed God and sought to do what was right. When he committed sin, he greatly repented.

David's Sin

David took interest in Bathsheba, the wife of a solider named Uriah. In order to take Bathsheba for his own, David ordered that Uriah be sent to the front of a battle at that the other solders fall back leaving Uriah alone to be killed. This was done and David then took Bathsheba as his own wife. The prophet Nathan pointed out through a story the sin that

CHAPTER 13: **David's Reign**

David had committed. David was immediately sorry for his sin and asked for God's forgiveness.

MAP ACTIVITY: DAVID AS KING

(Activity Book Page 111)

1. Locate Hebron and draw a crown here to indicate that this is the place that David was accepted as king of the tribe of Judah. It was over seven years before the other tribes accepted him as king.
2. Locate Jerusalem and write "City of David" here to indicate that David made this city his capital city and that it became known as the "City of David."

Activity Projects

COLORING PAGE

(Activity Book Page 109)

King David with His Harp
Color the picture of King David with his harp.

CRAFT PROJECT 1: KING DAVID'S CROWN

(save for use in Chapter 14)

Materials:
- ☐ gold poster board
- ☐ stapler
- ☐ craft gems OR markers
- ☐ craft glue OR hot glue gun

Directions:
1. Cut a 5 in. strip lengthwise from the poster board.
2. Decorate by gluing gems to the crown or by using markers to create your own gems.
3. Fashion around child's head and staple to the appropriate size.
4. Enjoy!

CHAPTER 14
The Israelites Under King Solomon

LISTENING TO GOD'S WORD

1 Kings 8:27-28

> But will God indeed dwell on the earth? Behold, heaven and the highest heaven cannot contain thee; how much less this house which I have built! Yet have regard to the prayer of thy servant and to his supplication, O Lord my God, hearkening to the cry and to the prayer which thy servant prays before thee this day

QUESTIONS FOR REVIEW

1. **When God asked Solomon which gifts he desired, what did Solomon ask for? Did God grant it?**

   Solomon asked for wisdom. Yes, God made him the wisest of all the rulers of his time. Besides wisdom, God gave Solomon the wealth, glory, and power that he had not asked for.

2. **How did Solomon decide the case of the two women both claiming the same child?**

   He tested the mothers by threatening death to the infant. The true mother was revealed in that she was willing to give up her child rather than see the child die.

3. **What took place at the dedication of the Temple?**

   At the dedication of the Temple, twenty-two thousand oxen and one hundred and twenty thousand sheep were offered in adoration to God. Solomon gave thanks and, after his prayer, fire came down from heaven to consume the sacrifices. People from every part of Solomon's kingdom came to the dedication of the Temple, staying with him and feasting for fourteen days.

4. How did Solomon protect his kingdom and his traders?

   He erected fortresses along the northern frontier and in the plains. He fortified the Temple and palace and built a city to protect his caravans coming in from the East.

5. What two major factors led to the break-up of Jewish unity?

   taxation and idolatry

6. How did Solomon forsake God?

   He worshiped false gods.

7. After he tore his cloak into twelve pieces, what did the prophet Ahijah tell Jeroboam to do?

   He said, "Take for yourself ten pieces; for thus says the Lord, the God of Israel, 'Behold, I am about to tear the kingdom from the hand of Solomon, and will give you ten tribes . . . because he has forsaken me . . .'"

8. What pattern do we see throughout the history of the Old Testament that still takes place today?

   Times of happiness and prosperity, followed by periods of decline due to man's sinfulness.

NARRATION EXERCISES

Solomon and the two mothers

Two women came before King Solomon both claiming to be the mother of the same child. In order to determine the true mother, King Solomon came up with a test. He said that the child should be cut in half and half given to each woman. The true mother said not to harm to child but to give it to the other woman. She loved the baby so much that she would rather give him up than see him put to death. In this way King Solomon determined who the true mother was and returned the child to his mother.

MAP ACTIVITY: SOLOMON'S TEMPLE *(Activity Book Page 117)*

1. Locate Mount Zion on the map. Draw one wall of the temple and label "Temple."

CHAPTER 14: **The Israelites Under King Solomon**

Activity Projects

COLORING PAGE

King Solomon and the Temple *(Activity Book Page 113)*

Color the picture of King Solomon and the temple which his father, King David, had designed and which he saw through construction.

KING SOLOMON CROSSWORD

(Activity Book Page 115)

Fill in the answers to the crossword.

Down:
1. Wisdom
2. hammer
3. blessing
4. Priests
5. Temple
7. slay
9. Sheba

Across:
3. bronze
6. Israelites
8. Gentiles
10. half
11. Covenant

ACT OUT KING SOLOMON AND THE TWO MOTHERS

Supplies:
  crown from Chapter 13 Activity
  baby doll or stuffed animal
  three actors/actresses

Directions:
1. Choose who will play the role of King Solomon and have them seated at a central location with the crown.
2. Use two other actors/actresses as the two mothers.
3. Use the baby doll/stuffed animal as the baby being fought over.
4. Act out the story.

CHAPTER 15
Jeroboam and Rehoboam

LISTENING TO GOD'S WORD

1 Kings 12:24

"Thus says the Lord, You shall not go up or fight against your kinsmen the people of Israel. Return every man to his home, for this thing is from me." So they hearkened to the word of the Lord, and went home again, according to the word of the Lord.

QUESTIONS FOR REVIEW

1. What did Rehoboam do to provoke a rebellion against his rule?

   He said that he would increase the people's burden rather than alleviate it.

2. Why didn't Jeroboam allow the people of his ten tribes to worship in the Temple at Jerusalem?

   He wanted the people to be loyal to himself rather than to God.

3. What happened when Rehoboam set an example of idolatry, just as Jeroboam had done, and the people followed it?

   Because of this idolatry, God permitted the Pharaoh of Egypt to invade the kingdom of Judah.

4. Why did Jeroboam's hand wither?

   It withered because he spoke against the prophet.

5. How did the prophet Ahijah know that the disguised woman was really the queen? What did he tell her?

   He knew she was the queen because God told him. The prophet said that her son would die, her husband would be rooted out of the land, and her people would be taken into captivity.

6. **What was the result of God's people being split between Rehoboam and Jeroboam?**

   Prosperity came to an end because neither king was strong enough to trade with other countries. Meanwhile, civil wars ruined great portions of the country. Great numbers of soldiers on the battlefield meant great numbers of men taken from the trades and agriculture as soldiers; many of these good men died. Scarcity of food and a high cost of living naturally followed.

NARRATION EXERCISES

Rehoboam and Jeroboam

Neither Rehoboam nor Jeroboam were good kings. Their struggle for power led to many hardships for the people. Civil wars ruined great portions of the country.

MAP ACTIVITY: JEROBOAM AND REHOBOAM

(Activity Book Page 121)

1. Locate the cities of Shechem and Jerusalem and, using a red pencil, draw a line between the two cities to show that Rehoboam went to Shechem to be anointed king, but because of his foolishness and arrogance he instead had to flee to Jerusalem to avoid being killed.
2. Now shade the land of Judah, the land Rehoboam ruled, in red.
3. Locate the land of Israel, the land Jeroboam ruled, and shade it blue.
4. Note that the kingdom that was united under David and Solomon became divided.

CHAPTER 15: **Jeroboam and Rehoboam**

JEROBOAM AND REHOBOAM WORD SEARCH

(Activity Book Page 119–120)

Word Search Answer Key

1. Rehoboam
2. Shechem
3. taxes
4. chariot
5. Jeroboam
6. false
7. Judah
8. Israel
9. temple
10. golden
11. Assyrians

CHAPTER 16
Elijah and the Prophet

LISTENING TO GOD'S WORD

1 Kings 19:11-12

And he said, "Go forth, and stand upon the mount before the Lord." And behold, the Lord passed by, and a great and strong wind rent the mountains, and broke in pieces the rocks before the Lord, but the Lord was not in the wind; and after the wind an earthquake, but the Lord was not in the earthquake; and after the earthquake a fire, but the Lord was not in the fire; and after the fire a still small voice.

QUESTIONS FOR REVIEW

1. **What did the prophet Elijah tell Ahad would happen because of his idolatry?**
   Elijah said there would be a great drought and no rain would fall for three years.

2. **At the brook, how did Elijah receive food each morning and evening?**
   God commanded the ravens to feed him there each morning and evening.

3. **When the brook dried up, where did Elijah go and who fed him? How did she have enough food for him?**
   Elijah went to Zarephath where a widow fed him. God sustained her food supply throughout the entire drought.

4. **What did Elijah do when the widow's son died? What did God do?**
   He prayed to God and asked Him to restore the boy to life. God raised the boy from the dead.

5. **How did the people come to believe that God was the one true God and not Baal? What happened to the prophets of Baal?**

   The fire of the Lord fell and consumed the offering. The prophets were put to death as the Lord commanded.

6. **How was Naboth's vineyard taken from him?**

   Jezebel had false accusations spread about Naboth and he was stoned to death. Ahab, the king, then took possession of the vineyard.

7. **How was Elijah taken to heaven?**

   A fiery chariot pulled by horses came and Elijah went up to heaven in a whirlwind.

8. **Name two miracles associated with Elisha.**
   - The general of the Syrian army was cleansed of leprosy.
   - The dead man, who touched Elisha's bones, came back to life.

NARRATION EXERCISES

Elijah, the ravens, and the widow

God told Elijah to go to a brook. There God commanded the ravens to bring food to Elijah every morning and evening. When the brook dried up, Elijah went to Zeraphath. There a widow fed him and God sustained her food supply. When the widow's son died, Elijah prayed to God and the boy was restored to life.

MAP ACTIVITY: ELIJAH CHALLENGES THE PAGANS

(Activity Book Page 129)

1. Locate Mount Carmel. Here draw an altar to the Lord with twelve stones, one for each of the twelve tribes of Israel. Draw a trench of water around the base and flames on top. This represents the altar that Elijah built proving that God is the one true god and not Baal.

2. Locate Beersheba on the map and draw and angel to indicate the place where the angel visited Elijah and fed him. Draw a line with yellow from here to Mount Horeb where Elijah went and lived in a cave.

3. From here draw a line with yellow to the wilderness of Damascus to show that Elijah, at God's command, went to Damascus.

CHAPTER 16: **Elijah and the Prophet**

Activity Projects

COLORING PAGE

Elijah Begging God *(Activity Book Page 123)*
Color the picture of Elijah begging God for the life of the widow's son.

The Fire of God from Heaven *(Activity Book Page 125)*
Color the picture of the Lord's fire consuming the offering as Elijah prays.

ELIJAH FINDS THE WIDOW MAZE

(Activity Book Page 127)

Help Elijah find the widow who takes him in and feeds him.

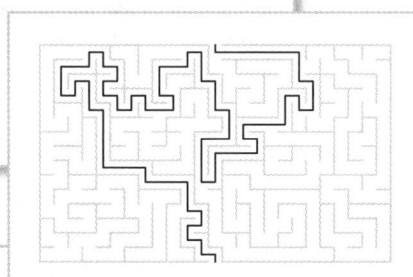

CRAFT PROJECT 1: PAPER PLATE RAVEN

Materials:
- ☐ 3 paper plates
- ☐ black marker
- ☐ scissors
- ☐ stapler
- ☐ googly eyes
- ☐ yellow construction paper
- ☐ black construction paper
- ☐ metal round paper fasteners

Directions:
1. Color all 3 paper plates black.
2. Leave one plate full size, cut the center circle from one of the plates and discard the outer ring, and cut the third plate in half.
3. The full size plate is the body of the raven.
4. Staple the small inner circle to the top of the full size plate. This small circle will be the head of the raven.
5. Use brackets to attach the half plates to the sides of the full size plate. These are the wings of the raven.
6. Cut a triangle that is 2 in. on each side out of the yellow construction paper. Glue onto the head of the raven so that one point faces down.
7. Glue the googly eyes above the triangle.
8. Use the black construction paper to fashion two feet for the raven. These can be small triangles with the point stapled to the body.

9. Use extra black construction paper to cut "feathers" to be stapled on top of the raven's head.
10. Enjoy!

CRAFT PROJECT 2: ALTAR AT BAAL PROVING GOD IS THE ONE TRUE GOD

Materials:
- ☐ white construction paper
- ☐ brown construction paper
- ☐ blue marker
- ☐ orange and yellow tissue OR construction paper
- ☐ craft or popsicle sticks cut into 3 in. segments.
- ☐ craft glue

Directions:

1. The white construction paper is the background for the altar.
2. Cut the brown construction paper into 12 rock-like shapes.
3. Paste the rocks in a pyramid formation hallway up the pieces of white construction paper.
4. Take the 3 in. segments of popsicle or craft sticks and paste them like logs on top of the rocks.
5. Draw a trench of blue water along the base of the altar.
6. Add small squares of crumpled tissue paper or construction paper and paste them to be the flames on top of the altar built to God.

SNACK PROJECT 1: THE RAVEN BRINGS BREAD AND MEAT

Ingredients:
- ☐ bread (any type desired)
- ☐ deli meat (any type desired)

Directions:

Today is a great day for a deli sandwich for lunch with a discussion of how the ravens were commanded by God to feed Elijah bread and meat at the brook.

CHAPTER 17
The Stories of Job and Jonah

LISTENING TO GOD'S WORD

Job 1:21

And he said, "Naked I came from my mother's womb, and naked shall I return; the Lord gave, and the Lord has taken away; blessed be the name of the Lord."

QUESTIONS FOR REVIEW

1. **Who did God allow to test Job? What limitation was put on this test?**
   God allowed Satan to test Job. Satan could not take Job's life.

2. **Name some of the things that Job lost as part of his trials.**
   Job lost his oxen, sheep, camels, dozens of servants, his children, and his health.

3. **How did Job please God? How did God show that He was pleased?**
   Job pleased God by his patience in suffering. The Lord showed that He was pleased with him by rewarding him. He restored Job's health, doubled his wealth, and gave him seven more sons and three more daughters.

4. **Why did God send Jonah to Nineveh? Why did Jonah head the opposite direction of Nineveh?**
   God sent Jonah to Nineveh because the people there were wicked and God wanted them to repent. Jonah headed the opposite direction because he was afraid of the cruel Assyrians.

5. **Why was Jonah thrown into the sea? How was he saved from the sea?**
   He admitted that he was the cause of the storm and told the crew of the boat to throw him overboard. A great fish swallowed Jonah and cast him up on the shore three days later.

6. **What did the people of Nineveh do in response to Jonah's preaching?**
   They fasted, put on sackcloth, and repented of their wickedness.

NARRATION EXERCISES

The Trials of Job

God found Job to be a very good man who feared Him and turned away from evil. God allowed Satan to test Job. Job lost his livestock, his servants, his children, and his health. Still Job praised God. Job was patient in his suffering. As a reward God restored Job's health and doubled his wealth. He also gave him seven more sons and three more daughters.

Jonah

God commanded Jonah to go to Nineveh. Jonah didn't want to go because he was afraid. Jonah went by boat in the opposite direction. God sent a great storm. Jonah told the crew to throw him overboard in order to calm the storm, which they eventually did. Jonah was swallowed by a great fish and then was cast up on shore three days later. Jonah then went to Nineveh where he gave God's message. The people of Nineveh repented of their wickedness.

MAP ACTIVITY: JONAH DISOBEYS GOD

(Activity Book Page 135)

Directions:

1. Locate Joppa on the map. In blue draw a line from Joppa out into the Mediterranean Sea.
2. Draw a whale in the middle of the Mediterranean Sea to indicate that Jonah was thrown overboard and swallowed by the whale.
3. Using blue, draw a line from the whale back to shore.
4. Now use yellow to draw a line from here to Nineveh. This shows that Jonah finally did what God asked of him.

CHAPTER 17: **The Stories of Job and Jonah**

Activity Projects

COLORING PAGE

Jonah and the Whale *(Activity Book page 131)*

Color the picture of Jonah being swallowed by the whale after being cast overboard during the storm.

SNACK PROJECT 1: CANDY TRIALS OF JOB

Ingredient:
- ☐ bag of candy-coated chocolates or other favorite candy

Directions:

Begin your story of trials of Job with, "Job found favor with God and received many blessings from him. Job was healthy and happy and glorified God." Place 2 candies before the child.

"Job lived in a house built of stone with his seven sons and three daughters." Place 10 candies before the child.

"He had many servants to wait on him." Place another 10 candies before the child.

"He owned seven thousand sheep, three thousand camels, five hundred yoke of oxen, and five hundred donkeys." Place 7, then 3 more, then 5 more, then 5 more candies before the child.

"God allowed Satan to test Job. Job lost all of his livestock." Take away 20 of the candies. Continue, "Job lost all of his servants." Take away 10 more candies.

"Job lost all of his children." Take away another 10 of the child's candies.

"Then Satan took away Job's health. Job was filled with sorrow and pain." Take away the last 2 candies. Place all of the candies out of sight.

"Job was ridiculed by his wife and friends and told his troubles were a punishment. Still, Job told his friends that even though he suffered greatly, he still trusted in God. In the end, Job held tightly to his love and faith in God. Job pleased God by his patience in suffering. So the Lord showed that He was pleased with him by rewarding him. He restored Job's health and doubled his wealth, and Job had seven more sons and three more daughters." Give back the candies in handfuls showing that God gave abundantly to Job because of his trust in Him.

CRAFT PROJECT 1: STYROFOAM CUP WHALE

(Activity Book Page 133)

Materials:
- ☐ styrofoam cup
- ☐ blue paint
- ☐ silver OR white pipe cleaner
- ☐ googly eyes
- ☐ stapler
- ☐ craft glue OR hot glue gun
- ☐ Lego figure or other small "man" figure
- ☐ Template from Activity Book

Directions:
1. Cut a small hole in the bottom of the cup (the pipe cleaner will thread through here).
2. Paint the entire cup blue.
3. Cut pipe cleaner into 6 in. segments and thread through the hole.
4. Set the cup face down on a hard surface (the rim of the cup is on the surface and the bottom of the cup is in the air with the pipe cleaner coming out of it).
5. Bend the pipe cleaner at the ends (this is the spray coming from the whale's spout).
6. Cut 2 fins and 1 tail out of blue construction paper to fit the size of the cup you are using. Staple the fins to the bottom sides of the whale and the tail to the back. Cut a mouth out of red construction paper and glue onto the cup.
7. Glue on the googly eyes.
9. Place the "man" figure under the whale.
10. Enjoy!

JOB CROSSWORD

(Activity Pages 137)

Fill in the answers to the crossword.

Down:
1. health
2. disasters
4. patience
6. blame
8. return

Across:
3. lightning
4. punished
5. Job
7. blessed
8. rewarded

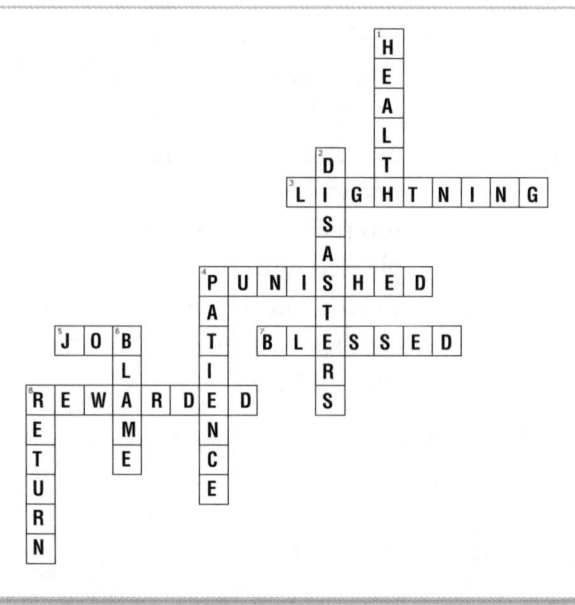

CHAPTER 17: **The Stories of Job and Jonah**

SNACK PROJECT 2: GOLDFISH CRACKERS

Today is a great day to have goldfish crackers alongside your Jonah and the whale craft.

SCIENCE PROJECT 1: SATAN TRIES TO PULL JOB IN

Materials:
- ☐ glass Erlenmeyer flask OR glass bottle with the opening smaller than body of the bottle
- ☐ water
- ☐ water balloon
- ☐ match
- ☐ scrap of paper

WARNING!
This experiment uses fire. Children should be supervised closely to avoid injury.

Directions:
1. Fill the water balloon with water to where it is slightly larger than the opening to the glass.
2. Light the paper on fire and place it in the bottom of the glass.
3. Place the balloon on top and steady it with your hand (while the flame is still lit the balloon will wobble as air is escaping around the sides of the balloon).
4. When the flame goes out, the balloon will be sucked into the flask.
5. To get the balloon out, blow into the glass. This will force the balloon to begin to come out of the opening. You can pull it out the remainder of the way.

In this lesson, the balloon is Job and the flame is Satan. Job does not allow the flame to tempt him. He does not allow the flame to burn in his life. Therefore he can rest easily on top of the glass bottle. If, however, he were to allow the temptation to take root in his life, it would push him in as the balloon is pushed into the glass bottle. Once inside, it's very difficult to get back out. We need to blow on the bottle in order to get the balloon back out (this represents God's help).

The physics behind this experiment: Warmer air takes up more space than cooler air. Once the fire is out, the air cools rapidly, thus condensing. This makes the atmospheric pressure outside the bottle greater than that inside the bottle. The balloon is therefore pushed inside the bottle.

PART FIVE
How God's People Went into Exile and Returned

CHAPTER 18
The Assyrian Invasions

LISTENING TO GOD'S WORD

Judith 16:13-14

> I will sing to my God a new song:
> O Lord, thou are great and glorious,
>   wonderful in strength, invincible.
> Let all thy creatures serve thee,
>   for thou didst speak, and they were made.
> Thou didst send forth thy Spirit, and it formed them;
>   there is none that can resist thy voice.

QUESTIONS FOR REVIEW

1. **Why did God allow the king of Assyria to invade the Kingdom of Israel and destroy the capital city of Samaria?**

   God allowed this because of the Israelites' sins of idolatry, dishonesty, murder, adultery, and oppression of the poor.

2. **What made Tobit noble?**

   He obeyed the Law of Moses and performed acts of kindness towards his fellow man.

3. **How did Tobit become blind and how did he regain his sight?**

   Tobit became blind when bird droppings fell into his eyes. He regained his sight through a salve made from the gall of a fish.

4. **How was the Assyrian army kept from capturing Jerusalem?**

   An angel entered the camp of the Assyrians and killed one hundred and eighty-five thousand soldiers. Sennacherib, the king, was so frightened by the slaughter that he returned to Assyria, never again coming after the Kingdom of Judah.

5. Who rebuked the elders of Bethulia for placing a time limit on God?
   Judith

6. Who killed the general Holofernes and how was this accomplished? What did the Assyrians do in response?
   Judith killed the general by convincing him that she wanted to help him capture her city. One night when he became drunk and fell asleep, she cut off his head and then returned to Bethulia. The Assyrians were panicked and fled to the hills, pursued by the army of Judah.

NARRATION EXERCISES

Tobit

Tobit was a noble man who obeyed God and was kind to his fellow man. He buried the dead who had been killed by the cruel king. He became blind when bird droppings fell into his eyes. He accepted his suffering. His sight was restored when the gall of a fish was used to make a salve and this salve was placed on his eyes.

Judith

Judith was a very brave woman. She rebuked her elders for putting a time limit on God. She promised to put an end to the battle and then she went to the Assyrian camp. There she told the general that she had come because she wanted to escape his attack. She waited and when the general became drunk and fell asleep, she cut off his head and then hurried back home. When the army discovered their leader had been killed, they fled.

MAP ACTIVITY: THE ASSYRIAN EMPIRE

(Activity Book Page 143)

1. Locate the Assyrian empire on the map. Using a red pencil, draw a line from the Assyrian empire to the city of Samaria in Israel, and circle Samaria in red to show that the Assyrians attacked and conquered Samaria.

CHAPTER 18: **The Assyrian Invasions**

Activity Projects

COLORING PAGES

Raphael, Tobit, and Tobit's son *(Activity Book Page 139)*
   Color the picture of the angel Raphael with Tobit and Tobit's son.

Judith *(Activity Book Page 141)*
   Color the picture of brave Judith with the sword she used to cut off the king's head.

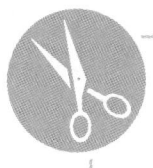

CRAFT PROJECT: JUDITH'S SWORD

Materials:
- empty wrapping paper tube
- 9 in. by 3 in. strip of cardboard
- aluminum foil
- scissors
- markers
- craft jewels (if desired)
- hot glue (if using craft jewels)

Directions:
1. Flatten one end of the wrapping paper tube and shape to be the point of the sword.
2. Cut a hole in both ends of the 9 in. x 3 in. cardboard piece. The hole should be just large enough to slip over the end of the wrapping paper tube.
3. Slip both holes onto the end of the wrapping paper tube that hasn't been flattened. This will be the hilt for the sword.
4. Cover the sword and hilt with aluminum foil.
5. Color with markers if desired.
6. Hot glue jewels onto hilt of sword if desired.
7. Enjoy!

CHAPTER 19
Daniel and the Babylonian Captivity

LISTENING TO GOD'S WORD

Daniel 2:20-22

"Blessed be the name of God for ever and ever,
  to whom belong wisdom and might.
He changes times and seasons;
  he removes kings and sets up kings;
he gives wisdom to the wise
  and knowledge to those who have understanding;
he reveals deep and mysterious things;
  he knows what is in the darkness,
  and the light dwells with him."

QUESTIONS FOR REVIEW

1. **What did Jeremiah prophesy about the people of Judah?**

   Jeremiah prophesied the evils that would come to the people of Judah if they relied on Egypt.

2. **What did Jeremiah do as a warning of what was in store for the people of Jerusalem if they continued their wicked lives?**

   He walked the streets of the city with a yoke around his neck.

3. **What did Jeremiah and some Levites do to protect the Ark of the Covenant?**

   While the Babylonians were plundering the city of Jerusalem, Jeremiah and some Levites secretly removed the Ark of the Covenant and the altar of incense. They carried them across the Jordan and hid them in a cave in Mount Nebo.

4. **How did Daniel clear Susanna of the crime of which she was accused?**

   He questioned her accusers separately. Their stories did not match, so they were found to be lying.

5. **What happened when Shadrach, Meshach, and Abednego refused to worship an idol?**

   Nebuchadnezzar had them thrown into a fiery furnace, but an angel of God protected them.

6. **Why was Daniel thrown into the lion's den? How did he keep from being eaten?**

   Daniel was thrown into the lion's den for disobeying the law that forbade him to pray. God sent an angel to protect Daniel and despite the lion's hunger, they did not harm him.

7. **What did the handwriting on the wall at the king's feast in Babylon mean?**

   It meant that all who were there would be punished for drinking wine from the sacred vessels that had come from the Temple in Jerusalem.

NARRATION EXERCISES

Jeremiah

Jeremiah warned that evils would come to Judah if they relied on Egypt. He walked the streets of the city with a yoke around his neck as a visual symbol. His prophecies came true. The sad sight of Jerusalem led Jeremiah to write the Book of Lamentations.

The Fiery Furnace

Shadrach, Meshach, and Abednego refused to worship an idol as King Nebuchadnezzar had commanded. For their punishment, they were thrown into a fiery furnace. They were protected by an angel of God and walked about freely in the furnace. When Nebuchadnezzar saw this he called for them to come out. Nebuchadnezzar then blessed them and their God.

Daniel in the Lion's Den

Daniel was thrown into the lion's den for disobeying the law that forbade him to pray. An angel of God protected Daniel so that the lion's did not hurt him. Daniel trusted in God even though he faced a den of hungry lions.

CHAPTER 19: **Daniel and the Babylonian Captivity**

MAP ACTIVITY: THE BABYLONIANS ATTACK JUDEA

(Activity Book Page 157)

1. Draw two red lines from the Babylonian Empire to Jerusalem to represent the two attacks on the city.
2. Beside one of the lines near the city of Jerusalem write the words "two years" indicating that the second attack lasted for two years.
3. Using yellow, draw a line from Jerusalem to Mount Nebo, showing that Jeremiah got the Ark of the Covenant out of the city.
4. With blue, draw a line from Jerusalem to the city of Babylon, showing that the captives of Jerusalem were taken to Babylon.

Activity Projects

COLORING PAGES

Daniel and the Lion *(Activity Book Page 145)*
 Color the picture of Daniel in the lions' den.

CRAFT PROJECT 1: FIERY FURNACE PAPER BAG

(Activity Book Pages 151–155)

Materials:
- ☐ Templates from Activity Book
- ☐ popsicle sticks OR straws
- ☐ colored pencils
- ☐ paper lunch bag
- ☐ clear tape

Directions:

1. Color Shadrach, Meshach, Abednego, and flames from the template found in the Activity Book.
2. Cut out the figures and flames.
3. Tape the figures to the popsicle sticks.
4. Cut a circular hole in the middle of the paper lunch bag.
5. Tape 3 flames around the opening of the hole.
6. Turn the bag upside down. Tape 3 more flames to the new top of the bag. Put figures in through the opening of the bag. Use the popsicle stick figures to show them walking around in the fiery furnace.
7. Enjoy!

CRAFT PROJECT 2: DANIEL AND THE LION WOODEN SPOONS

(Activity Book Pages 147–149)

Materials:
- ☐ 2, 10 in. wooden spoons
- ☐ Templates from Activity Book
- ☐ small piece of neutral fabric
- ☐ brown yarn
- ☐ markers
- ☐ colored pencils
- ☐ hot glue gun

Directions:
1. Cut out and color Daniel's body from Activity Book. Hot glue onto the spoon.
2. Cut a small scrap of fabric and fashion over top of Daniel's head. Hot glue into place.
3. Cut a piece of brown yarn to wrap around the cloth hat.
4. Use markers to add eyes, nose, and mouth to Daniel.
5. Cut out and color the lion's body from the Activity Book and hot glue to the second wooden spoon.
7. Cut as many pieces of 1–2 in. brown yarn as you can fit around the face of our lion and hot glue them into place
8. Use markers to create eyes, a rectangular nose, and scary teeth.
9. Enjoy!

SNACK PROJECT 1: FIERY FURNACE S'MORES

Ingredients:
- ☐ graham cracker squares
- ☐ regular size marshmallows
- ☐ mini chocolate bars
- ☐ little bear graham crackers
- ☐ aluminum foil

Directions:
1. Preheat oven to 350 degrees F.
2. Place graham cracker squares on a foil lined baking pan.
3. Place a mini chocolate bar on top of the graham cracker.
4. Place a regular size marshmallow on top of the chocolate bar.
5. Bake in the oven for only a minute or two. Watch for the marshmallow to start to expand and look toasty.

6. Add 3 mini bear graham crackers to the center of the marshmallow. Attempt to stand them up. These are Shadrach, Meshach, and Abednego walking around in the fiery furnace.
7. Enjoy!

CHAPTER 20
The Prophets

LISTENING TO GOD'S WORD

Isaiah 53:4-6

> Surely he has borne our griefs
>   and carried our sorrows;
> yet we esteemed him stricken,
>   smitten by God, and afflicted.
> But he was wounded for our transgressions,
>   he was bruised for our iniquities;
> upon him was the chastisement that made us whole,
>   and with his stripes we are healed.
> All we like sheep have gone astray;
>   we have turned every one to his own way;
> and the Lord has laid on him
>   the iniquity of us all.

QUESTIONS FOR REVIEW

1. List the four Major Prophets.
    1. Isaiah
    2. Jeremiah
    3. Ezekiel
    4. Daniel

2. What did a prophet do?
    He foretold the future and told the people what they must do to please God at the present time.

3. **List some of Isaiah's prophecies.**
   - the coming of Christ
   - the passion and death of the Savior
   - the establishment of the Church

4. **What book did Jeremiah write that described the destruction of Jerusalem and the suffering of his people?**

   the Book of Lamentations

5. **What type of message did Ezekiel give? Who was it addressed to?**

   Ezekiel's message is one of hope and of victory, saying that God will be true to His promises and deliver His people. It was addressed to both the Jews left behind in Jerusalem and to the Jews in captivity in Babylon.

6. **What does Ezekiel's vision of four living creatures symbolize?**

   The symbols of the Four Evangelists, or Gospel writers, come from this vision. St. Matthew is represented as a man, St. Mark as a lion, St. Luke as an ox, and St. John as an eagle.

NARRATION EXERCISES

The Prophets

The prophets were men of God who both foretold the future and told men what they were to do at the current time to please God. The four Major Prophets were Isaiah, Jeremiah, Ezekiel, and Daniel.

Activity Projects

COLORING PAGE

Prophet *(Activity Book page 159)*

Color the picture of the prophet of God and decide which prophet you think it is. Write the name of the prophet you have chosen on top of the coloring page.

CHAPTER 20: **The Prophets**

PROPHET CROSSWORD PUZZLE

(Activity Book Page 161)

Fill in the answers to the crossword puzzle.

Prophet Crossword Puzzle Answer Key

Across:
- 4. Nathan
- 5. John
- 6. Samuel
- 9. foretold
- 11. Jeremiah
- 15. Christ
- 16. Daniel
- 17. Church

Down:
- 1. spoke
- 2. Mark
- 3. Passion
- 7. Luke
- 8. messenger
- 10. Matthew
- 12. Ezekiel
- 13. Isaiah
- 14. Elijah

CRAFT PROJECT 1: A RAM'S HORN

Materials:
- ☐ party blower
- ☐ brown construction paper
- ☐ brown yarn
- ☐ brown marker
- ☐ rubber band
- ☐ stapler
- ☐ hole punch
- ☐ hole punch reinforcements

Directions:

1. Roll your construction paper to create a funnel shape. The small end of the funnel should just barely fit the party blower.
2. Staple the funnel into place and trim the end so that it creates a smooth circle.
3. Place party blower in small end of funnel and secure with the rubber band.
4. Hole punch 1 hole in the wide opening of the funnel and attach hole punch reinforcements around the hole. Color them brown to match the construction paper.
5. Cut a piece of yarn long enough to attach to the party blower end and go through the hole punch with enough slack that the child can wear the horn over his shoulder.
6. Enjoy!

CHAPTER 21
The Return to Jerusalem

LISTENING TO GOD'S WORD

Nehemiah 8:10

> Then he said to them, "Go your way, eat the fat and drink sweet wine and send portions to him for whom nothing is prepared; for this day is holy to our Lord; and do not be grieved, for the joy of the Lord is your strength."

QUESTIONS FOR REVIEW

1. **In what ways did Cyrus act favorably toward the Jews?**
   - He issued a decree that permitted all the Jews from the Kingdom of Judah to return there.
   - He gave back to the Jews the sacred vessels that had been taken from the Temple by King Nebuchadnezzar.
   - He gave orders for the Temple to be rebuilt.

2. **Why did many of the Jews remain in Babylon after they were permitted to return home?**

   The journey back was long and dangerous and they had made a home for themselves in Babylon.

3. **What did the returning Jews do as soon as they reached the city of Jerusalem?**

   They built an altar where they could offer sacrifices to God.

4. **How long did it take to rebuild the Temple after the first cornerstone was laid?**

   It took twenty years.

5. **What brave action did Esther take to help save her people? What was the king's response to this action?**

    She approached the king and spoke to him without being invited to do so which in those days was punishable by death. The king, instead of being angered, was very pleased with Esther and offered her even half his kingdom.

6. **What was Haman's punishment for spreading lies about the Jews and deceiving the king?**

    He was hanged on the same gibbet that he had prepared for Mordecai.

7. **How was instruction in religion provided to the people who had returned to Judah?**

    Ezra built synagogues where the people could gather and listen to the Levites read the scriptures.

8. **How long did it take to rebuild the walls of Jerusalem? How was this accomplished so quickly?**

    It took fifty-two days and was accomplished so quickly because every Jewish family was assigned a certain section of the walls to rebuild.

NARRATION EXERCISES

Esther

Esther was chosen to marry the king of Persia. Esther was a Jew. The king's chief advisor, Haman, plotted against the king. Mordecai, Esther's uncle, discovered the plot but did not know Haman was involved. Mordecai told the king and this angered Haman. In turn, Haman spread lies about the Jews to the king. Esther needed to do something to save her people, so she approached the king and spoke to him without being invited. In those days, that was an action punishable by death. Esther was very brave to do this. Esther held a dinner for the king and for Haman. There she exposed Haman for the liar he was. She pleaded for the lives of her people. The king believed her, and Haman was hung on the gibbet he had built for Mordecai.

CHAPTER 21: **The Return to Jerusalem**

MAP ACTIVITY: THE PERSIAN EMPIRE

(Activity Book Page 165)

1. Write "Cyrus" in between the Mediterranean Sea and Persia to indicate that he ruled over all of this land.
2. Using yellow, draw several lines from Cyrus' empire to Judah, showing his decree that all Jews could return to the land of Judah.
3. Draw some yellow circles inside Cyrus' empire, showing that many Jews chose to stay since they had made homes and lives for themselves.

Activity Projects

COLORING PAGE

Queen Esther *(Activity Page 163)*
Color the picture of Queen Esther.

CRAFT PROJECT 1: A CROWN FOR QUEEN ESTHER

Materials:
- ☐ gold, silver, pink, purple, or any desired color poster board
- ☐ stapler
- ☐ craft gems OR markers
- ☐ craft glue OR hot glue gun (You may find that hot glue allows for more vigorous play.)

Directions:

1. Cut a 5 in. strip lengthwise from the poster board.
2. Decorate by gluing gems to the crown or by using markers to create your own gems.
3. Fashion around child's head and staple to the appropriate size.
4. Enjoy!

CRAFT PROJECT 2: A ROYAL SCEPTER FOR QUEEN ESTHER

Materials:
- ☐ 1, 3 in. polystyrene ball
- ☐ 1, 12 in. thin dowel
- ☐ aluminum foil
- ☐ craft gems
- ☐ hot glue gun
- ☐ non-washable markers in desired colors

Directions:
1. Attach the dowel to the ball by simply pushing the dowel into the ball.
2. Wrap the ball and dowel completely in aluminum foil.
3. Color the scepter any color desired.
4. Attach craft gems with hot glue gun if desired.
5. Enjoy!

CHAPTER 22
The Last Days of the Kingdom of Judah

LISTENING TO GOD'S WORD

2 Maccabees 12:43-45

> He also took up a collection, man by man, to the amount of two thousand drachmas of silver, and sent it to Jerusalem to provide for a sin offering. In doing this he acted very well and honorably, taking account of the resurrection. For if he were not expecting that those who had fallen would rise again, it would have been superfluous and foolish to pray for the dead. But if he was looking to the splendid reward that is laid up for those who fall asleep in godliness, it was a holy and pious thought. Therefore he made atonement for the dead, that they might be delivered from their sin.

QUESTIONS FOR REVIEW

1. **Who defeated the Persians? What empire gained control of the land that the Persians had conquered?**

   Alexander's armies defeated the Persians, and the Greeks conquered the Persian's land.

2. **What happened to Heliodorus when he insisted that the treasure of the Temple be handed over to him?**

   No sooner had Heliodorus entered the Temple than a heavenly soldier, dressed in golden armor and seated on a horse, appeared to him. The soldier was accompanied by two other young men, beautiful and strong and glorious in appearance. The horse rushed on Heliodorus and, striking him with its front hooves, knocked him to the ground. Then the two young men stood on either side of the fallen man and whipped him furiously.

3. Name some ways that Antiochus Epiphanes tried to force the Jews to worship the gods of the Greeks?
   - The Temple of the true God was made into a temple of the false gods so that pagans went there to worship their idols.
   - In all cities of Judah, pagan altars were set up and pagan worship was required.
   - Anyone who followed the laws of the Jews and who observed the Sabbath was punished by death.

4. Eleazar knew that even if man could be deceived, God could not; therefore, he refused to take what action?

   Eleazar refused to pretend to eat pork in order to escape death at the hands of Greeks.

5. Why was the family of martyrs killed in such a terrible way?

   They were killed for refusing to eat pork, which would have been a transgression of their religious laws.

6. Even though the Jewish forces were greatly outnumbered, Judas went with confidence into battle. Why did he have such confidence?

   He had a vision in which the high priest Onias and the prophet Jeremiah appeared to him and promised victory.

7. With whom did the Jews make an alliance? What did they gain from this alliance?

   They made an alliance with Rome and gained Rome's protection.

8. Who was appointed as the king of Judah?

   Herod the Edomite

NARRATION EXERCISES

Heliodorus

Heliodorus attempted to steal the treasure from the Temple. When he entered the Temple, a heavenly soldier, dressed in golden armor and seated on a horse, appeared to him. The solider had two younger-looking men with him. The horse rushed on Heliodorus and knocked him to the ground. Then the two young men whipped him.

The Family of Martyrs

Seven brothers and their mother were all ordered to eat pork, but this would have been against their religious laws. They all refused. The king had them all tortured in a most terrible way. The mother cried out to her sons to be strong and to accept death. They knew it was better to obey God and die than to disobey him and live.

MAP ACTIVITY: THE MACCABEES

(Activity Book Page 167)

1. Locate Mount Zion and draw a line in blue from Mount Zion to Jerusalem to show that Judas Maccabeus led his army from Mount Zion to Jerusalem in order to meet the attacking king of Syria.
2. Locate Syria and draw a line in red from Syria to Jerusalem to show that the Syrian king came to Jerusalem to attack the city.
3. Draw two more red lines from Syria to Palestine to show that Antiochus Eupator, the king of Syria, sent two armies to attack there.
4. Circle Palestine in blue to show that Judas Maccabeus won the battle there.

Activity Projects

CRAFT PROJECT 1: TREASURE CHEST

(to signify the treasure Heliodorus tried to steal)

Materials:
- ☐ shoe box
- ☐ yellow construction paper
- ☐ black construction paper
- ☐ craft glue
- ☐ gold-covered chocolate coins
- ☐ any leftover craft gems from other projects
- ☐ black marker

Directions:

1. Completely cover both the lid and the bottom parts of the shoe box with the black construction paper by gluing the paper onto the shoe box.

2. Cut 2 in. thick strips from the yellow construction paper to fashion a boarder all along the edges of the treasure box. Glue this border on top of the black background, covering every edge.
3. Take a rectangular piece of yellow paper and write the words "Temple treasure." Glue this to the middle of the treasure box.
4. Cut a small 2 in. square from the yellow construction paper and hand color a "key hole" with a black marker.
5. Fill the box with the chocolate coins, craft gems, and other any items you wish.

Acknowledgments

Creating the Teacher's Manual for *The Story of the Bible* was a large project, made possible by many talented and generous people.

Thank you to the many moms, teachers, church groups, and others who generously shared their ideas and creativity, in person and online. For Story of the Bible, I drew inspiration in particular from: www.bibleschoolteachers.blogspot.com, farmfreshadventures.blogspot.com, artistichandsoffaith.com, 123homeschool4me.com, and gluedtomycraftsblog.com. The puzzle generators at discoveryeducation.com, crosswordlabs.com, and mazegenerator.net were valued resources as well.

I thank the Saint Benedict Press team for all of their hard work and dedication in making this project come together, including: Mara Persic, art director; Caroline Kiser, graphic designer; Nick Vari, production editor; and Morgan Witt, editorial intern.

Lastly, I would like to thank my family for all their love and support. My children, Aiden, Mary, Patrick, Peter, Jude, Paul, Teresa, Imelda, David and Annie are a daily source of inspiration for me. Without them this book would not exist. And Conor Gallagher, my publisher, is also my husband. I love you, Conor, and am blessed beyond measure to have you as both.

TAN Books was founded in 1967 to preserve the spiritual, intellectual and liturgical traditions of the Catholic Church. At a critical moment in history TAN kept alive the great classics of the Faith and drew many to the Church. In 2008 TAN was acquired by Saint Benedict Press. Today TAN continues its mission to a new generation of readers.

From its earliest days TAN has published a range of booklets that teach and defend the Faith. Through partnerships with organizations, apostolates, and mission-minded individuals, well over 10 million TAN booklets have been distributed.

More recently, TAN has expanded its publishing with the launch of Catholic calendars and daily planners—as well as Bibles, fiction, and multimedia products through its sister imprints Catholic Courses (CatholicCourses.com) and Saint Benedict Press (SaintBenedictPress.com). In 2015, TAN Homeschool became the latest addition to the TAN family, preserving the Faith for the next generation of Catholics (www.TANHomeschool.com).

Today TAN publishes over 500 titles in the areas of theology, prayer, devotions, doctrine, Church history, and the lives of the saints. TAN books are published in multiple languages and found throughout the world in schools, parishes, bookstores and homes.

For a free catalog, visit us online at
TANBooks.com

Or call us toll-free at
(800) 437-5876